This Special Life and Me

and

Me

Based on a true story, my journey and some of my experiences I share.

TERESA ANN

BALBOA.PRESS

A DIVISION OF HAY HOUSE

Balboa Press books may be ordered through booksellers or by contacting:

Balboa Press
A Division of Hay House
1663 Liberty Drive
Bloomington, IN 47403
www.balboapress.com
844-682-1282

Because of the dynamic nature of the Internet, any web addresses or links contained in this book may have changed since publication and may no longer be valid. The views expressed in this work are solely those of the author and do not necessarily reflect the views of the publisher, and the publisher hereby disclaims any responsibility for them.

The author of this book does not dispense medical advice or prescribe the use of any technique as a form of treatment for physical, emotional, or medical problems without the advice of a physician, either directly or indirectly. The intent of the author is only to offer information of a general nature to help you in your quest for emotional and spiritual well-being. In the event you use any of the information in this book for yourself, which is your constitutional right, the author and the publisher assume no responsibility for your actions.

Any people depicted in stock imagery provided by Thinkstock are models, and such images are being used for illustrative purposes only. Certain stock imagery © Thinkstock.

Print information available on the last page.

ISBN: 978-1-5043-8248-9 (sc)
ISBN: 978-1-5043-8289-2 (e)

Balboa Press rev. date: 10/19/2020

My gratitude goes to all who encouraged and supported me writing and finishing this book. I would like to thank Kathy, Cheryl, James, Jessica, Ro, Brenda, Sheri, Debbie and my mom (a very special lady) for the countless of hours they spent editing. They edited this book but did their best to leave the way I speak intact. They felt it was important for the reader to see me as an individual; I have learning disabilities and include some of this journey in the book. My gratitude goes to Elizabeth, who used one of many of her talents in the drawing, which can be seen on the back cover. (The front and back cover is a glimpse what I was gifted in seeing while up in Heaven.) A special thanks to my loving son and family. I will remain always grateful, thank you all from the bottom of my heart, love you all!

This book is based on a true story!

I have revised this book and also had added more inside the book since was published back in 2017.

Based on a true story, my journey and some of my experiences I share.

"This Special Life and Me"

This special life is given to all of us. Our perception sometimes clouds the way we view it. We all have a story to tell, and this is mine.

I am sharing some very special awesome experiences I encountered with both God and Jesus. The experience was not only for me on a personal level, but for others!

One of many special precious moments was from my first memory and was with God. I was under one year of age when I began recalling past memories of my own spiritual journey with God and Jesus. One experience I had just laid down in my bed resting my eyes, still very much awake. Only moments passed and I turned to my personal relationship with God and Jesus. I dared to ask of them a very special favor and was answered. I was given the gift of my request! One special beautiful experience I share in the book when I am much older. I asked Jesus to see my dad whom had passed within four months prior. I was brought there not once, but twice. I experienced going there two completely different ways! Yes, I was wide-awake both times!

My Journey starts out with God. Included in this journey, I experienced two traumas, which sent me back and both times God and Jesus were with me. I am one of many that are sharing a spiritual and somewhat of a personal journey of my life with God and Jesus. Jesus was with me in the waking hours and God was with me as I laid my head down to sleep. How my relationship unfolded due to a trauma early on and how they guided me through like a parent went. They dealt with me through my early years, as well as adult years and that is on a more personal level. The same as a parent does or should do, while I was adjusting, growing as well as learning, of being amongst others here.

Chapter 1

While with God
I make a discovery

Following conception within the womb of our mothers, we did dwell and grow, awaiting the moment to experience a journey on earth amongst others like us.

As for all of us, our life began prior to our very first memory. For some of us however, our first recollection or our earliest memories had a depth of impact that either we cling to willingly or attach ourselves to involuntarily. Those memories can linger, and even stay with us for years or even possibly throughout our life's journey on earth. It can impact us, be it a good or bad memory, from that moment forward and influence us as we grow past the actual moment. When discussing either our first or earliest memories, we are reconnecting to the child still within us, of course only momentarily during reflection.

We might bring up these earliest memories from time to time, if it was a good or special memory. I had one of those special first memories. I hold my first memory dear as it was a wonderful start in my personal relationship with God and Jesus, which has grown from that moment on. I will share some of my journey I experienced with them. One I share in the book, at a very young age (around age three or four), from a trauma I experienced, I turned and asked Jesus to become an adult figure for me, (like a parent figure), and he did just that!

Looking back upon my very first memory, in many ways defines who I am today. My passions awakened for understanding and discovery. I learned from the importance of paying attention to detail, can possibly bring about deeper understanding. There are possible discoveries both on a personal and spiritual level. My Journey begins by exposing a huge discovery while in the presence of God. My concern of losing these moments with God; knowing they were precious was due to my young age and knowing that I could easily forget. The solution I came up with was repeating how I have to remember these moments as they passed through my thoughts each time. It worked and I remembered all of it!

My first memory

Before I share my first memory, I first wish to describe some important details. My family and I were sitting on a pew in church. Where we sat was in the back section of the church, nearest to the main center aisle. My mother sat to the right of my dad, who held me on his lap, and my two older siblings sat to our left. I noticed there were more folks near the front of the church, only some were in the middle section and it was emptier where we sat on this day. Sharing the same bench on the far end left of us; I spotted another family with one son sitting nearest to the wall of the church.

My first memory as I recall, began when I looked from my mom and then to my brothers to the left of me, while being held on my dad's lap, I spotted this small family sitting further away sharing our same pew. Past this family, was the interior wall and I spotted on that wall several crosses and a man's image carrying them. I instantly recognized this man on these crosses as Jesus and acknowledged who he was, God's only Son! How I understood this and the crosses and that it was Jesus is unbeknownst to me. What I had no knowledge of was the impact of why Jesus was carrying those crosses. Jesus' journey that led up to this, which I later learned is called the Stations of the Cross. I didn't stay focused on Jesus carrying these crosses for very long, instead I looked directly upward, sensing God's strong presence. My thoughts returned to my dad momentarily, supporting and holding me up on his lap. I understood in this moment that I needed his arms holding me up. I saw my siblings were capable of sitting on their own and that is what made me aware of this very thing. I was very young, probably around one year of age or under. Following my heightened awareness that my dad was holding me, I returned my thoughts to God's presence and believed in this moment I was in the audience with him. I didn't see him, but I felt him, and recalled that I was comfortable with this. I began to speak to God through my thought method only. I just believed he could hear me from within and there were no barriers or separation between us. I am not sure how I came up with this but during these moments I grasped this barrier did exist between me and my parents and all others.

I was feeling God's strong presence very near and because of this I was inspired to converse with Him. This question is what popped into my thoughts. "So, you're my daddy's father and you're my father"? (I have no recall prior as to why this question came to mind, other than possibly my two older siblings may have mentioned God is our Father in Heaven.) I waited a moment, but God didn't speak instantly. I took it as I needed to be the one that had to answer my own question before Him and that He was waiting for me to seek this answer within myself. Moments later I said, "Yes". I do recall feeling slightly confused by my own answer; apparently I was seeking an understanding that was vitally important for me in this moment. I sought this answer from God, being I had his attention. From this point on, I associated God as Father to all. Only moments passed, still feeling his strong presence near when another question popped into my mind. "Why am I here and how do I get back?" Again, I waited a moment and again God didn't speak. It was just like the first time. I had to answer my own question. What I came up with was; I have to do good things in this life. Only I couldn't grasp what were these good things. I recall I paused and looked downward becoming somewhat confused in not knowing, didn't know what good things were exactly at this time because I was too young. I reasoned the answer would come later, as I grow and through God and Jesus. They will teach me those things and let these thoughts drop. I also grasped my older siblings were doing things I have yet to learn which only confirmed this. My first discovery came about letting those thoughts drop. It dawned on me that I was speaking clearly, using words in my parent's native language, only through my thought method. I acknowledged a second later that I have never spoken outwardly and that I didn't know how this comes about. I became all excited and to me this was a huge discovery and a secret. God's presence was still felt, only I was processing while before Him. My thoughts turned to, "How does one speak out loud? What is all this process? Nothing came to mind while I was figuring this out on my own. However, I did ask God, "How does one speak out loud?" I waited a moment and this time was relieved God didn't speak because it began to scare me a little. If I learned of this process that God had spoken what would happen?

I knew this was God's turf and He had the answers, even at this young age. My resolve was that I reasoned when it is the correct time during the growing process, it will come about and I will learn also to speak, as my two siblings were capable of also showing me this. I returned to my discovery, which made me feel excited once again and said I have to remember all of this so when I do learn to speak outwardly, I will share my secret discovery with my two older siblings. I spoke clearly the words within, using my thoughts only and shared my first audience and my questions I asked to God. I said this at least twice within my thoughts. All the while in the presence of God, I have to remember all of this. I was afraid I might forget and it did concern me, knowing I was so young and this could easily occur. I did remember all of it, which now at this late age I share. I have no recollection what happened prior and after. Later, I do recall when I could speak, making the decision not to share with my brothers my secret. I was a girl in their eyes and they were boys. I picked up on the fact that I didn't fit in their club this early on!

Chapter 2

I began retaining some more memories around the age of three

One memory was the birth of my younger brother and I had recently turned three years of age. I recalled my grandmother was watching us and we were sent to bed, only I didn't go to sleep because I was awaiting the phone call since I was praying it would be a sister. When the phone rang, I snuck out of my bed and walked partly into the dark hallway and overheard my grandmother speaking loudly. All excited, she said, "another boy". I turned away and went back to my bed, sad and recalled while walking back to my bed I became upset with God that He had brought us another brother. I let go of being upset quickly and accepted my younger brother with open arms. At this time of age, I was experiencing a typical normal relationship with both God and Jesus, which carried into the present, my first memory. Sometime past, these things take a major change and gratefully so. Having known of them prior, I became dependent upon them, though not in your typical common normal form.

Chapter 3

The first trauma

At around age three or four years, my world turned upside down. A couple of young girls nearby were making fun of me over something I just did and was too young to understand their reaction. I believed I had done something wrong, that is all I am going to mention on this. However, during the moments following, I became frightened when emotions came over me that I didn't get or understand (went into shock). Those feelings that came over me were foreign. They remained in my young reasoning and I thought that some areas within my brain had stopped working, as prior were fine. From that moment forward, I believed those areas now are harmed (or lost to me) within my brain of me having access to using. I attempted to approach my mom, and recalled vividly walking up to her as she sat at the table, only I couldn't find the words to put together to speak, so I turned away from her with my head down. I felt completely lost, frightened and now very much alone (fell into despair). I went into the den and sat alone in my thoughts and recalled my first memory, and this time I turned to Jesus instead of God, yet knowing both He and God knew what all just occurred.

The moment I inwardly called out to Jesus, I felt His presence enter the room. This brought me comfort feeling no longer alone. Knowing He knew therefore, I wouldn't have to find words to speak it, also He knew my present thoughts which were obviously not the case that I lost some areas in my brain, yet I believed I did. Jesus didn't speak, although I had hoped He would, but this was familiar to me because of my first experience I had with God where He didn't speak and I instantly accepted this was how it would continue moving forward with Jesus during these next moments with Him being so near. I didn't rehash all that just happened before Him, only I projected my future ahead of me. How long will it take for all of this to become clear (fixed, so to speak), all I saw was a dark cloud hovering as I projected me growing older and seeing this darkness remain. I understood this as, it will be some years that I will remain in this state of confusion and feeling lost. I recall I became angry (this emotion I was familiar with and didn't traumatize me) that I was brought into this terrible, frightening state, and shared this with Jesus. I quickly accepted what all now I had to face ahead of me moving forward. My thoughts returned towards knowing I wasn't alone going through all of this. My comfort knowing Jesus and God were with me.

While still feeling Jesus' presence near, I realized I was much too young and felt at this moment I lost my mom, or rather I felt my mom lost me, because a separation had now occurred, unbeknownst to her. I felt cut off from my mom (to a degree) from this point forward. I recognized at this young age I was much too young to take this on alone with all that taken place; the worst being my new concerns that some areas were harmed (lost) within my brain as well, turning to my mom to helping me. I somewhat lost my mom and understood I needed an adult figure in my life that could understand what all I had just encountered to help me while I grow and get past this. At this point, I somewhat understood Jesus once lived on the earth, so being I still felt Jesus' presence remaining near while I sat, I asked Him if He will become this adult figure (was my wordings and how I reasoned back then, was being like a parent figure to also raise me while here on earth). Although Jesus didn't speak, I didn't feel His presence leave following asking Him this, and just believed He accepted. He did!

I grew accustomed through my first memory that God didn't speak through a verbal method or on other memories at that time and I carried this same reasoning growing forward now with Jesus, somewhat now raising me. I accepted I wouldn't be verbally spoken to at that time; however, over time this does change as I grow.

Like my first memory, I felt God's presence, I felt Jesus' presence always nearby and was literally a thought away (like a phone call away) just like with a parent being close in connection with their young child hovering nearby. I turned and spoke inwardly with Jesus, mostly during the daytime if need be which became often through my early years. God the Father was during bedtime where I would reflect upon my day with him, and all the while felt either or presence. I was growing with having accountability in my own behavior, so to speak, during my reflecting moments with God and I was slowly learning what all was pleasing in His eyes. It was I who began, from the beginning, separating each Jesus and God early on, where God was during bedtime. I still needed both present in each day and an established relationship continued forward as I continued growing. I felt completely connected and was reliant upon each of them from that point forward in my personal relationship with each of them while in my daily life amongst family and others. I believed Jesus will guide me to what I needed to grow to learn regarding this trauma occurrence and this did happen.

I am jumping ahead some years. I mentioned earlier this dark cloud I envisioned did come to pass and all this confusion didn't become resolved until I was either in fifth or the sixth grade. That was a long stretch of time gone by and already adapted to my relationships I been having with both Jesus and God, (not knowing of any other to turn back towards). Not a thought entered my mind where now what I had known having with them would change, instead things remained as they had been. All this while, I still moved forward growing within my home environment and turned to my mom for other things, only this void of her not knowing for me formed a separation until I was able to approach her. First, I reached most in understandings by this point (regarding that earlier trauma) and found the words easily now to speak out to her. I never shared the entirety of all I had gone through with her at that time; only a little but felt this was enough. These thoughts never entered my mind for me to share with her how I once believed how I was harmed in some areas in my brain or being I was so young I could not communicate any of it with her. I also didn't mention to her I turned to Jesus and asked Him to step in as my adult figure in helping raising me. All my family ever did hear through the years is Jesus' and God talks to me, never a thought popped into my head to share with them why this came about and yet I always believed we are loved equally in the eyes before them. I also didn't share with her (my mom) at that time till now how I first thought I would be learning. Once I entered kindergarten, and the huge crisis following when this didn't occur (I will share momentarily). When this revelation hit home, for me the emotions I felt, (earlier trauma) and not areas in my brain instantly thought I lost, I felt a sense of relief. So this dark cloud I had seen ahead (as years) came to pass, because I was much too young to process these difference emotions and areas of the brain. I recalled thinking now I could learn more easily, but this wasn't the case because I was still struggling when it came to learning, period.

In the next few chapters I am discussing my school years.

Chapter 4

Misconceptions of Kindergarten partly explain why I became lost

My first memory left an impact on me in many ways and remained as like my paper trail in defining also who I am to me. I would revisit this memory at times throughout my life. I began kindergarten; I was still four years of age soon to be turning five, (so please keep this in mind). In my first memory, I didn't know yet this *process* in how one speaks out loud; I couldn't identify or explain how this would come about. Here I could let it go because this made me feel overwhelmed. My way with reasoning didn't change much from my earliest memory. Once I began school, my assumption of what all I would be learning first was way off base. Thinking I would begin learning the *process* when using areas within my brain, like their names and what they could or should be doing. Basically, what these areas that I should be doing while using them does for me, "the process." I believed all this would be introduced at the very beginning and once knowing now this knowledge, I would be ready to learn such as letters, numbers etc… in those lines through my teacher. In my young reasoning, I recall prior to my first day starting school, I couldn't figure out how I would be taught by my teacher and what she would be using to accomplish this teaching of "the process," I hadn't a clue. What could have helped me is being presented *associations* I could relate to so I could learn it. I had a wrong interpretation of what kindergarten would be from the get go. From my earliest memory of entering into kindergarten, my awareness and how I reasoned didn't change, as far as getting "there's a process and using areas within the brain that are part of the process". I became silent and a sense of doom came over me. Once I discovered my teacher was not going to do any of this, I also had another reason for wanting to know about these areas. I might spot and link some areas I believed I had lost. I could turn to my mom with names of these areas and mention they are no longer working for me and she could help me fix it or get me the help in fixing it. This never came about. Emotions and areas within the brain are totally separate, yet in my young reasoning I was stuck with were areas of the brain, not emotions, for some years to come.

I felt lost in this environment when my teacher began teaching her way and was picking up my peers and they were excelling and I wasn't. I became shutdown. I recalled midway into this year while in class talking inwardly with Jesus; I was trying to reason as to why I didn't learn the areas within the brain, as I once thought upon entering school at the beginning. This reasoning still remained in my thoughts. I mentioned to Him maybe it is best I didn't learn them at the beginning and that maybe this could have frightened me explains why this didn't come about. However, I still picked up I still needed some sort as the likes of further input in order for me to feel capable with learning, because

I still felt very lost in this environment, period. Outside of school I was fairing much better, only because I wasn't experiencing this shutdown nor having to comprehend this learning process that I needed to be using. Around this same time shortly following where this realization hit me, I was in deep trouble due to the fact that I didn't understand enough about the process in which I so desperately needed to move forward in order with learning new things through school, (triggered a different form of a shutdown), a new issue arose only this was even much more serious. I couldn't hold onto and carry a thought within using verbal thought form method; not even to converse with Jesus inwardly and it became impossible to accomplish. This disturbed me greatly on top of all else that I was experiencing. I still felt Jesus' presence near, thankfully, which did comfort me, but still, back then I was in a bad way and was aware of this very thing.

I had no voice to speak of, no examples presented in which to help myself during my early years in school. I had nothing offered through how to relate through different examples (on paper) read to me by my teacher, where as I can point to (or later going back to, where I needing to process this information of insight just read). With me making this connection in spotting and seeing my issues I was experiencing, therefore I remained stunted. There was nothing offered where I could make some form of a connection where I might then could attempt to somehow recreate it for future learning. Basically, I was shutdown often while in this learning environment and it grew worse than better. I couldn't even carry a thought within. Eventually, past kindergarten, I came up with a solution to somehow converse with Jesus inwardly during school, but it was not through a verbal method as what I was accustomed to doing earlier while in school. (I basically was spotting the problem and problem solving.) Jesus wasn't offering these answers verbally, instead by feeling His presence, I knew I had to solve these issues I was experiencing and that He would show me how instead of speaking it out through a verbal communication. I thought I had to be diligent in looking for clues that come my way and I trusted Jesus would aid me in spotting these.

I began problem solving and I share the solution momentarily.

Overall, during this time I was growing with learning through experiencing these valuable qualities, trust and patience and through feeling His presence near showing me love. I recalled during bedtime, I would reflect on my day before God and I was not only inwardly verbally talking as much but, was using a different method, (visual method, unbeknownst to me what this method was or called at that time) and would recall remembering much of my day during my reflection moments with God.

Throughout a day, between me and God at nighttime and Jesus during the daytime helping me, I certainly was learning not only trust but patience and above all else love. What these truly mean and what I was also taught was honesty and accountability for my own behaviors and actions, as I was growing. Basically, all it was is what was pleasing in God's eyes. (Recall how I would spend time during bedtime with God and revisiting my day with him, I began using this method to also help me figure out multiple things, be it a problem or a situation that had arisen at school or at home. This was accountability I was referring to for myself before God, as well of course Jesus, and also my moments to being open to spotting solutions that could come up.) I spent much time focused on now trying to fix this major issue where I couldn't even converse with Jesus, as well me carrying a thought; I came up with my solution.

I attempted using this same visual method as I used with God to converse with Jesus in school and this began working.

Whew! It had taken some time, but it did begin to work. Being this became my main focus, I now shut down. Dealing with my other issues about how to figure out how to grow in this type of teaching through school had taken a back seat, so to speak. However, looking back, it started out with this learning through school that left me stunted and over a short period of time, being it wasn't corrected, causing this huge shutdown to eventually having occurred to begin with. Eventually, I was able to return to using a verbal form (this was a long process) with Jesus while at school, but by this time, I also now was comfortable using this visual method and began using both forms. I began inwardly speaking more through verbal, along with using visual form with God. During bedtime was like my first memory with him. During this stretch of time, outside of being in this environment (school), I fared much better in the home environment because I was able to carry a thought, as well inwardly to speak (verbally) with Jesus much more easily. I wasn't shutdown in my home dealing with learning things as I was in school.

I need to mention there were other lessons I needed to be getting that didn't pick up explaining the reasons Jesus didn't just speak it out verbally to me. These answers I so desperately felt I needed for me to learn through school and share in the book.

Although I fared better once home, I also had the same results occurring while in school. It was during religion class that also started up around the same time I was beginning kindergarten. I already was having serious issues exposed to me with growing outside of my home since starting school and these serious issues that surrounded me while learning carried over into this environment as well. I wasn't adjusting in either of these environments. The thought never occurred to me to speak of any of these issues I faced to my mom. I only turned to Jesus. Although on top of the same struggles I was experiencing when in school, I was also experiencing other issues that I couldn't identify back then. This was all somewhat conflicting for me in my young reasoning. One, *I* wasn't learning about my parent's past during my young years of them raising me. This was confusing to me as I was learning about Jesus, especially while His presence was felt in the room. I was not taught Jesus by my parents. Therefore, it became difficult to comprehend, at least at this point. I was dependent upon Jesus as being my adult figure, helping me in those present moments surviving while growing forward through a day-to-day basis. Thereafter, He was the rock that I leaned upon.

As the years passed, I still held onto hope and shared this with Jesus. Sometime down the road, I will become capable of learning just as my peers did. I was shown how easily I could learn more about Him and His life here on earth, as soon as I figured out how it was that I learn. I believed He heard me and felt confident that what I did know at that time was OK. I never felt pressured by Him. The only pressure I found was what I put on myself as I grew through the years. I was still struggling with how it was that I would learn best and how I would answer my huge dilemma about learning. I would easily become distressed throughout my religious education just as it was with school and this wanting to learn remained. If only I just could grasp in how it was taught then maybe I would be able to learn for myself.

A perfect example of exposing how little I was capable of learning due to my conflict I was having with learning about Jesus and also my learning disabilities, while in religious classes. Somewhere, I overheard Jesus being called Jesus Christ early on, but how I had taken it stuck for years. I was thinking that Christ was His last name. I kept missing that part with hearing, Christ meant the Son of God, the Messiah. I knew from my first memory that Jesus was the Son of God, so this wasn't the issue. It came down to either I wasn't capable due to this conflict or I couldn't process information due to my learning disabilities. It was both reasons that were going on during religious classes. Looking back in my young reasoning, I wanted to be respectful so when I called to Jesus inwardly, I always said Jesus Christ. Christ as I was thinking of being His last name. As always, I instantly felt His presence near me. He chose not to correct me rather He showed me His love and His protection through His mere presence while I was continuing to be near Him. When I did figure it out, much later in time, about what Christ really meant, I giggled at myself while in His presence. I was grateful for that time he allowed me grace to discover this at my own pace and on my own.

I picked up that He was taking baby steps with me, referring to my growing with learning through a religious educational environment, as well as in a school environment. What I also caught was that He was teaching me to begin to think on my own; although He is with me, I needed to discover this very thing. I was so connected with Him and God so early on that I was in union with them always. Although, I was doing this, I was "getting it not getting it" sort of thing back then. Something else I had taken from this experience (I thinking Christ was his last name) was another affirmation that He will bring me to where whatever it is I need to learn and or possibly seek was in the reason and that is in my personal reasoning. Another important lesson was I still had to remain aware (diligent) looking for the clues He will present to me to the spot referring to me about this whole learning issue I been dealing with, period. What this presented was for me to stay in the present in means of referring to awareness in what all is going on around me.

Another huge turning point, a clue, presenting a means about how I can retain information and begin growing with learning about God as well Jesus came about through my dad, whom was very big on watching religious movies. Early in my years I was exposed to these. Eventually, I began to watch when they were on TV. Two movies stood out for me that held my focus, "Moses" and "King of Kings". Granted, I was in my home environment, but also both movies had a special interest for me, being one the movie "Moses" was exposing some more about God and the other "King of Kings" was about Jesus. Here I could grasp the process and retain easily, yet I was baffled for some time to come as to why, how, I could retain the information. Every year, these movies would return to our TV screen and I would learn a bit more each time I would see them.

This is where I grew in my learning. Basically, this was my religious educational period. With what I took away from these movies and learned, I had gained enough awareness in what I needed, as far as my religious education and I recalled that I spoke of this with Jesus. I just got to a point as I aged that whatever I might hear, while in my religious education (as like in school) I was loosely referring to retaining shortly when the teacher was speaking. I easily lost my place and my awareness with spotting my problem. The issue was still there about how to retain information because no one had taught me this process and I was left to myself to figure out how to understand a learning environment, period. In religious education, I was being taught through similar means as I was taught in school. They were using verbal and book presentations and I didn't do well with this format. I couldn't store information into my memory. These two special movies were visual with verbal where I did my best receiving new information with learning and I was able to grasp process and retain the information.

When my time was with God in the evenings, unbeknown to me back then, what I was applying was the visual method along with verbal thought methods, which was video like imagery. While I was rehashing, I would see it as a video from things that had occurred that day and I would discuss it with God. Therefore, much later in my life, I grasped it when I was seeing these two special movies. They had both clicked for me as being they were similar. They were familiar to how I had been processing, visual and applying video format during processing and retaining new information. Although I been doing this sort of thing unconsciously, like using video imagery and was it most natural, I begin "getting it, not getting" it sort of thing during the years later. Basically my later schooling years I was still experiencing this problem. Still, it was long after school that I fully got how it is I process information best.

How it began as I recall from my first memory with God, I would rehash these special moments in time. I would see that by applying my video imagery processing with God, I would be able to retain for a day's time period. This was not happening during learning through the learning environment method. I also began interpreting what I had seen. For example, while rehashing all of the day in what all I did store, (without understanding how I was doing it); I knew I would be discussing my day with God come evening. Trying to be as honest I could and then speak about it with God, I was able to discover my own faults in using this method, so to speak, and learn from it and work on my failings.

This presented a means first with having accountability while in God's presence. It was during this form of method processing that seemed to work. I began using it for all things in my early years, while me coming up with solutions. I would use this throughout my school years. Yet it was very difficult, as far as retaining textbook information or when the teacher was giving instructions, especially if spoken fast. However, this area never resolved itself.

How I processed information was creating difficulties because being in a school environment or religious education was in the moment and what little I did pick up would be rehashed while in the presence with God. I missed so much learning. When I was little, I went along and that is why I learned some because I had taken what I did learn to God and then I moved slowly forward with learning. This also explains why it was easier in my home than me being in a learning environment. I was using this method unbeknownst to me about the process and retaining was impossible for me to be using in school or religious education. I didn't figure it out and "get it" that I was doing this very thing until much past my school years. Subconsciously, I tended to analyze (not always) what it is I see. Over the years, I have grown fast in using how I process information the best. I felt like an outsider in both places (school and religious education) through my young years and had feelings of frustration with my lacking of how to process information. God was always nearby, everyday while I was moving forward.

I picked up something at one point watching "King of Kings." What I had picked up was spotting Jesus mentioning that God is to be addressed as Father and this prayer Jesus brought to the people back then and was to be passed on through the generations known to this day is the "Our Father's Prayer". Hearing this resonated with me and became excited I knew of this one, because of my first memory with God while I was trying to understand and asked him if he is Father to my dad and Father to me. I did eventually learn "Our Father's Prayer" and how long it had taken for me to retain it. I can't recall, but I was determined to learn this prayer. I recall through one of those times seeing the "King of Kings" movie, that was where it eventually clicked that Christ was another name for Messiah and wasn't His last name. Around this time, I began putting a face to God with His presence I had always felt. It was in this face, He had a lot of gray hair, but I had never seen His actual face, only what was His presence that I felt. Then at some point, I had grown and reasoned that Moses didn't see God's face and at some point I focused more on God. With His presence felt while I was in prayer, I was reflecting with him over my day. I also gave Jesus a face to go with when His presence felt nearing, although He never revealed His face. In my young reasoning, He (Jesus) had once had a face because He once lived and walked on earth among others and taking from the movie of His life, "King of Kings," here I saw a face and began placing this face with Jesus' presence and continued doing so for some years to come. Neither God nor Jesus reprimanded me that I had attempted placing a face on them, confirmed of this was their presence that continued being felt when I was speaking with them, even past this stage of me doing this. Sometime in my young years it dawned on me that I had brought this question to God where I didn't see either of their faces this whole while. God didn't answer nor reveal either of their faces to me. Although I had hoped I would receive this huge blessing, still I was somewhat nervous if I had seen, being I was so accustomed to relying on feeling their presence. All the while I just trusted they knew best and let this issue drop. Sometimes I would catch myself returning to my childhood faces that I had placed on God as well Jesus while speaking with them and I feel that this was OK.

Chapter 5

My silence remained another lesson in itself

I wish to take a few moments and share some things referring to all my school years and things I had to learn while attending school, all the while with Jesus nearby and come evening be sharing my experiences with God.

Before I begin, I mentioned that it never dawned on me to turn to my mom during my struggles with learning mainly because Jesus was present and I felt it was left up to me about figuring out my issues and the difficulty with learning I was experiencing. That factor made me feel alienated at such a young age and turned to Jesus as a parent figure, never thinking to turn to my mom about my struggles outside the home. I felt it was up to me in figuring it all out. Otherwise, she would have attended these environments from the "get-go," therefore this reasoning form stuck. This reasoning continued each day forward. Attending first Kindergarten as well as religious education and it explains why I never turned to my mom with issues outside the home, be it of my peers (social) or my learning disabilities and struggles.

At the end of kindergarten, my mom mentioned that my teacher had recommended I "redo" kindergarten and she asked if I wanted to do this. I instantly said no. I recalled thinking the last thing I wanted was an additional year added onto this nightmare, when I only had twelve more years to look forward to having to go through. This was my reasoning at this time and I had no problem with getting projection even at this young age, just as like in my first memory with a real concern I could easily forget being I was so young. I was put into first grade but it was called a "slow" first grade class. I was put into regular second grade and I don't believe they had a "slow" second grade class back then. I was learning, but at a much slower pace than my peers. I still was having some shutdowns where I couldn't retain a thought, but I was growing comfortable in this environment. Other types of shutdowns persisted that prevented me from learning because I was still stuck in not "getting the process" and how one retains information was not being taught. Odd as it was, basically one of my biggest dilemmas, I continued to face, was the absence in the knowledge of how I "processed information" and what I came up with so early on is that I didn't grasp it at all. How was it that I was learning those little things along the way and that I can apply it with learning new things, the steps, so to speak? I never knew enough on the "process", this discovery or experiencing this self-discovery is how best I could learn this sort of thing for my first few years of grammar school. Instead, I was aware of my lacking and how it was causing me to remain silent for my first few years of school. I recall with my second grade teacher, I felt a positive connection with her that I didn't feel with my other teachers. I can't recall her name, but she was really nice to me and I felt comfortable with her and recall feeling hope for the first time with learning. What was it that

I was lacking about learning started coming easily, but she was pregnant and left to have her baby. She didn't return to finish the school year and my hopes got squashed. The new teacher I didn't make this bond with.

Chapter 6

My relationship with Jesus and God grew

Another issue I did pick up while during school hours was spotting that I was lacking when I was with my peers. Sometime in third grade, I began acclimating myself in this environment and although my main issues continued of struggling, I felt I grasped what was expected while there. Around this time is when I began putting more focus on my issues with my peers and wanting to somehow fit in. I caught that they not only were doing well in learning but also were growing socially where I wasn't doing well. I recall I eventually came up with, they must have had this thought flow occurring within going on to explain why they were advancing socially; where I spotted nothing was going on within me in the moment. I was aware I was developing much slower than my peers, period. I needed much more input even when being around my peers and this I also did pick up. Jesus began talking with me literally, or that I became aware He was at this point in time. I was in third grade and it was during recess at school, I asked Jesus something (overhearing what other kids talk about) were two questions. "What is my favorite number," He said, "7". Then I heard Him speak with a deep masculine voice this number seven within. I was excited that now I have my own favorite number. My second question I asked immediately following, "What is my favorite color," he didn't offer this answer. I don't know if I frowned outwardly, but I did inwardly for certain. Therefore, I knew I had to figure this answer out for myself, as like in the past had shown me, because this time He didn't answer. Jesus was not only guiding me but I caught that He was teaching me to think on my own, so to speak. So, without delay, I answered it for myself all this while before Him, and came up with the color after thinking of some colors I was familiar with and chose the color red. Again, I became excited because this time I found this answer on my own. I felt as if I have a ready answer if ever asked either of these two questions, now I have a ready answer and might feel like I fit in, so to speak. As well, I could ask these questions to a peer and might get asked back same questions and would have an answer. OK back tracking, this first time I recall that I had heard Jesus speak verbally was a relief and was totally awesome! This was a huge turning point, as well as a growth spurt, for me in my relationship with Jesus and also with God when they communicated with me and me with them. There were times I wasn't conversing with Him and felt His presence (Jesus) coming near and I waited and within a moment He would speak. Hearing him inwardly, like the first time if he was intervening, just as a parent does for their young child if needing to intervene. When He spoke for the first time and I heard his deep masculine voice, an authoritative tone, I instantly attached this same voice to Him from that point on. When He spoke, He always was very direct, using very few words and it was usually on a personal level. As time went by I came up with a reasoning I thought this was why He spoke little words, that there was no room for me to misinterpret what was spoken, or where I could take it multiple ways and become confused.

Funny, how I kind of caught much of my lacking yet spent much focus on trying to fix everything. Like the second question I asked and Jesus didn't answer and caught comprehending I had to figure it out for myself, this was more how my days normally would go, only once in a while Jesus now might speak. God was using another method (not verbal like Jesus at that time) and would point things out to me during my reflecting using a visual and overtime I began to catch this very thing, and this continued to grow where he would intervene in this method for me.

My innocence reveals my unawareness of the powers of the Holy Spirit.

At one point God also began using a verbal method along with what I first was most familiar coming from Him was through a visual. Much later He also began only using a verbal at times. When I did pick up God was also using a verbal method, I spotted what was as of the same voice as Jesus. I instantly became confused and it dawned on me that I had yet to talk with both of them at the very same time. Well, I tried to do this very thing and I found I couldn't do it, which only made it much worse. Looking back, early on, I separated both of them; so to speak, in their rolls in how I needed each of them. This explains that I couldn't deal with it of having visuals from God plus verbal form from Jesus going on at the same time. I recalled it was evening time while with God when I became conscious of this very thing, in that I couldn't connect with both all at the same time. The moment all of this though had hit home, it became a serious crisis for me. I fell into this and I began pacing in my dark room stressing out. I was a mess for only a few days. When this happened, I think I was in either the fifth or sixth grade. Why this serious confusion? It only lasted a few days before I came up with a solution with each of them, which was keeping everything as it was. Jesus I relied on him during the day through evening and come bedtime was my time spent with God. I had continued to keep things of the same being and this was basically all I now knew up until then with both God and Jesus.

I needed more time to process this new reality and eventually came up with a solution and began gradually talking with God during the daytime. I eventually excepted the voice was of the same, only when I spoke with Jesus it was coming through him and when I spoke with God it was coming through God. The voice I learn much later was through the Holy Spirit.

Chapter 7

Finally while in school I received a breakthrough

I share only some important lessons I learned which helped me with learning, although still carrying issues I was having. I was using a visual (as well verbal) method within through means of communication both with God and Jesus, yet in my early years never put it together to be using this same method to learn. Just as I knew I was in for a long haul for those answers I needed from my trauma, I picked up this learning knowing it will be another long haul, but believed Jesus would present clues for me and that I had to be ready to spot them when they are nearing. Granted, wouldn't it had been awesome if told from the get go how it is best I learn from either of them, however, looking back I am grateful they didn't because I gained some ownership in it after spotting a huge clue where I came up with some ways to somehow recreate some of what I first spotted for me to learn and that did help.

I was gaining confidence and courage while putting forth the effort while using my reasoning to figure things out, although

Jesus always felt was nearby. Back then, I was not seeing it as I do now and I would easily fall towards frustration, only to have to once again pick myself back up and try again. With what all I did gain through spotting from this one time where a huge clue finally was presented. Not only was it able to bring me to focus properly, but using both my eyes and hearing together to not only grasp in the very moment but capable of retaining while tuning out any distractions I had issues with.

Sadly, in looking back, as I mentioned, I never had a thought to turn to my mom and share any of this with her nor with my on growing personal relationship having with both Jesus and God until I was years older (I shared some). I trusted Jesus would expose clues and help me grow and that He did. I spotted while conversing with Jesus moments prior, having this feeling that something wonderful is about to be exposed to me, only I had to come out of my comfort zone and gain courage is what it would take and was one of the most difficult moments I experienced in my young life.

Thankfully it came about and was through my teacher, Mr. B…, (I believe was my fourth grade teacher, yet could have been my third or fifth grade teacher). During class he handed out a sheet of math problems for each of us to do during class, after finishing going over one problem while he stood up front, instead of the norm he remained at his desk. He went and sat in the center of the room amongst us at one of our empty desks. He stated as he walked to this desk that if we have any questions to come to him there. Naturally, I needed help. This was a given, but apparently I was never taking the initiative to seek out his help prior. I did attempt doing some math problems, then became stuck shortly past starting, instead of getting up and standing on the growing line to receive his help, my anxiety rose and I remained glued to my seat. I recalled talking with Jesus but through a visual method this whole while, all the while trying to understand basically my hesitance, which also was filling me with anxiety.

I discovered one reason quickly. It was my fear of bringing attention to myself, being I felt lacking in many areas, be it with learning or should I have to speak to another child while in this line or with my teacher, (overly concerned I might shutdown becoming speechless or I might not get my words out properly to match a thought and being capable to explain myself clearly). This brought my attention to my confidence I so lacked, but my words and thoughts fell upon courage that I felt didn't have. I realized this was an opportunity where I could now try and conquer my fears. I watched as the others began standing in that line receiving the help and went back to their seats. When I got the nerve up, there were only two students waiting in line and I saw the other students were busy working on their math sheets. I felt it was now or never sort of thing and needed to gain this courage. The moment I stood up, (deep down knew I couldn't turn back or else I felt doomed) I began having a panic attack (although at the time didn't know what these feelings were that just came over me, yet knew it was related to my nerves and prayed to Jesus I wouldn't pass out as my heart raced and my breathing became affected some). I made it to the end of now short line, reminding myself over and over to take courage and needed to stay in this line, period. Another child lined up behind me moments following which made me feel somewhat calmer, (though not entirely). Why I found it calming, I didn't choose to analyze this at that time and excepting in that moment only just that it did and let that thought drop for the moment, knowing I was in a crisis mode to begin with. Thankfully, I didn't have long to wait as I stood in this line.

Once it was my turn, he didn't look up at me, oddly but this also relieved me, (my breathing now returned to normal instantly, my panic episode left.) He had taken my paper from my hand and looked over it and began doing the math equation on the paper speaking lowly, as well using only some words. Mainly I watched, but heard him speak and followed what he spoke while looking at my paper, which he asked me to grasp and retain (as I stood in front of him). He did ask me to step to his side at one point and I did, but by this moment I was already calm and was focused on the paper in his hand instead of the interference of multiple issues of which I could not name at that time. I was excited by how I was finally grasping something new that was being taught and it was coming about so easily. He gave me a different math problem but was using this same reasoning to go and do by myself, yet I felt a feeling of connection was made and spotting through using my eyes. More so while him doing the very math problem I was stuck upon I could make a connection, as well I grasped and was capable to easily now retain it. I walked light footed back to my seat. Several clues to several issues I became aware in this short moment spent watching on with him, yet needed time to process during outside of school. I already picked up some moments prior to ever standing in that line, but more revealed was centered on me and processing with learning.

One issue, which had taken longer getting, was something about me. If I was facing the front of the classroom and doing so this would throw me off and would shut me down. Part of explaining this was my awareness levels around me were increasing along with what I caught prior with my struggles having added "fuel to the fire" so to speak, was negative distractions making me even more self-conscious. Another reference to being in the classroom was him standing in the front of the room or sitting at his desk brought about moments prior to getting in that line with those issues I mentioned had my attention, but that I could identify through words those issues mentioned as I prior couldn't. Only this time, once I moved closer to his side, I found being I was calm, I could remain focused (I found a place to place my eyes), and because I could remain focused found easiest with comprehending while him doing this math problem I could not first get.

When it was time to leave for the day, he called me to the front and said to me quietly, with a smile "I am so proud of you for coming to me earlier for help." I just smiled! This was a huge turning point and I spent many hours be it with Jesus or God with trying to take in what I just discovered and try figuring out how I could repeat this for future learning. I felt hope. I was finally capable of learning something. It was coming about easily and I found it was through this unique form method. I was getting it! It was through more so using my eyes and not getting it sort of thing that I need visuals with learning. Possibly, I had auditory processing issues when it came to being in this environment because to have this discovery duplicated identically sadly it was not forth coming. Using both my hearing and eyes were difficult factors with overcoming (I share more on this shortly).

For me, this was the biggest breakthrough I so desperately needed in coming about which also occurred at school. I gained so much with all these few short moments it brought. I would go over these short moments many times as I grew through my school years and would spot new things I didn't spot prior. My first clue spotted was of me using my eyes and looking at the math equation being done. I found this made it easier to process and retain (yet other factors were part of this which helped me to grasp all of what he was doing outside of me thinking only was me using my eyes).

However, my first solution was that I needed to somehow come up with a strategy to mimic that moment I had with Mr. B… where I was using my eyes. I was trying to take a verbal and translate into a visual. On my next day at school, I came up with an idea and tried that while he spoke at the front of the room, I would read his lips. I was using my eyes and I found in doing this, it was working. I could process what he was saying. I thought I can finally learn. Doing this presented for me some sort of a visual through using my eyes where now I could connect to and lock in what it was he said. Unbeknownst to me, I had a severe issue referring to focusing and "getting and not getting" this for years to come. Yet, here in reading lips, I had a center point where I could focus while using my eyes. I was capable of hearing some better while reading his lips. Granted, if what he said went over my head, I obviously would become lost and would shutdown. While creating using a visual to lock into, was me learning to use my hearing to process as well while in school where this appears more so me having a problem with. Today, I still can have some issues at times with my hearing and processing.

I was given much insight and the discoveries I made had come forth from that precious moment in his classroom (and share these shortly). However, also did this moment bring attention to several issues I had referring with learning? It taken longer (years) for some of these issues to either spot while reflecting on these precious moments as I grew or picked up at the time or shortly following that moment and began to figure out how to deal with and resolve those. A couple issues were of me using both my eyes and hearing more so was while I was in this learning environment. I picked up the very ways I was conversing with God and Jesus all along was through a visual or verbal method but discovered that I am in need of using and applying sort of like these same things with learning. I wasn't introduced to what I knew I needed (the process) back then and these other ways (more traditional) that one picks up and uses with learning. I had to discover a different pathway to grow with learning. However, once I spotted this clue which was filled with many insights to my issues with learning, my journey to discovering new methods in order to get this grasping, retaining sameness effect to come about from that moment forward in a learning environment (school) finally began. Another huge lesson I was "getting not getting" sort of thing was I needed to reach out to another human being. Because I was mainly going to Jesus or God and yes, I did turn to my mom for different matters, such as things goings on within the home.

My first few years were "tell-tale" signs that I needed for further intervention than what I had at that time. The efforts of teachers were more so unsuccessful, due to the fact that I was very slow with grasping and because I needed to learn more about the process. At best, I needed some form of an introduction phase. First, to have had to come about and open me up to be capable to express myself now that I learned these new words (terms) I could use, whether I was or not still grasping, I would have had words to express this. Instead, I couldn't communicate and remained silent from that point forward.

Around sixth grade, I finally approached and asked my mom what my kindergarten teacher said I might have (as a diagnosis type). She said she was told that I was slow. I said that's it! Well, that was nothing. I could work within letting me know "do I or don't I" have learning disabilities? Not long after, I grew and passed my resolve moment occurrence in school as I continued, moving far faster. For me to catching up and my religious class got more structural in reading and studying scriptures, I still was struggling to retain much from either learning environment. I really was starting to believe I might have complications learning. This began weighing on my mind more, I kept flip flopping with this idea for years. It taken many years to except these complications I did have on top of early trauma was learning disabilities.

Over the years, I uncovered the many issues I once had with myself, if using my eyes and will repeat some, because I have other points I need to present. For starters, my focus if looking forward to the front of the classroom, I found highly intimidating and uncovered multiple issues explaining as to why. This is partly with me with using my eyes, as well my hearing. I wouldn't look at someone in the eye for several reasons. One reason, I felt they could see my confusion or lacking through my eyes. Another was my fear. This would be an invitation for another to communicate with me, be it teacher or a peer and my lacking skills in either about how this process works. Along with, I could become speechless (shutdown) or I might stumble over my words as I attempted to take my thoughts and try to relay these thoughts occurring within using the speech method. If looking downward, I would avoid this "whatever to come about" is what became my solution. But it would open me to possibly hear somewhat better. I began discovering, as I grew older, to pay more attention to how this was actually helping me and using this method more so with peers. Another issue exposed from this experience journey, much later picked up (years) was me, using my eyes if I looked into another's eyes too long, it becomes blurry and this blurriness shuts me down and will not allow me to focus. I recall I didn't know where to put my eyes basically. Downward, I found also worked best to solve this issue. I couldn't multi-task with using both my eyes and hearing well. While I was using my hearing, I was also having serious issues with and I became overly self-conscious with using. Perfect example was in the lunchroom, I learned early on through some of my peers that when they began whispering loudly around the table, I could overhear them and it made me feel highly uncomfortable (my consciousness levels with awareness are now much higher than my norm amongst my peers) and caused me to fight, not to hear, which was impossible to accomplish. I didn't get this "tune-out" thing. In these moments (which continued occurring) it brought attention to me. I was getting that I had to learn to "tune-out" and also to not feel I was doing anything wrong should I overhear (this took a long time getting, but eventually I got it). As well, where to place my eyes in these moments brought attention to me and was another reason I was having issues with using my eyes (yet it only enforced this behavior for some time to come because I placed them downward). I did begin to spot that once home, I fared much better amongst my family and friends, and this disturbed me as to why I struggled in other environments with using my eyes. Eventually, I discovered (years passed) on my own looking into the one eye method process, instead of trying to look into both eyes at the same time and found this finally worked best with peers, but still it was hard to do with a teacher. Could be because of distance? I still was encountering issues coming through my teacher, being I would be learning something through a teacher and I still didn't have all the pieces I needed for getting why I struggled with learning. However, this was difficult in doing. When it came to learning, I still picked up that I needed a focus point to center my eyes upon (like the chalk or eraser on the blackboard tray) so, I could better focus. This method helped in doing better with tuning out whatever it was adding and blocking me with learning.

This teacher (Mr. B…) touched my life immensely from that very moment. Not only in all of what it presented for me to continue to learn from it as I continue to grow, but it exposed him to doing what he did and was also about him thinking how to reach and teach me. This was making this sort of human connection. I once felt lost back in second grade and felt this connection come about once again! Another important detail that I need to mention is that I was ready to get the information and I had to start helping myself. When I was in school, the resources were not forth coming as they are today when referring to learning disabilities. Back then they didn't have these diagnoses about other diagnoses that are well known today. Once in middle school, all they had were Study Skills, and guidance counselors and they had slow learning classes and still they were clueless as how to help me. I caught early on that I had to help myself referring to learning. Jesus was still not speaking these answers, so instead I realizing that I already had the keys to fixing all this. I knew I had to keep seeking and He would place clues for me to spot, which made me become more aware that I had to spot when these clues came. Looking back I see it, He (Jesus) was bringing about my attention to seek first and raise me higher in my own awareness levels. I had to trust, as well to get out of my comfort zone, in seeking help through another human being and many other things I learned through this one experience. The lessons I needed to get would take many years.

I continued returning to all that I could spot in that precious moment I had with Mr. B...,. Some things I did pick up and began working on all by myself, just following that moment with Mr. B..., I had taken from this early on what he showed me doing this math problem. This had helped me see how it was I was to do it independently. I did ask if I could be taught this way, asking my guidance counselor, although sadly this couldn't be taught in this way. Heck, I could have had a different problem following, is how I thought. However, the solution I formed in using my eyes watching on, and attempted to duplicate this in a way where I can retain what is being said. I began reading my teachers lips where I knew there was a focus point. This helped me put his words into a visual but I still would become lost if too much was said or it was spoken too fast or the information went over my head and I could not grasp the idea. This teacher didn't speak fast and I was able to follow along while he was speaking. I began forming this "reading his lips" method to process the lessons but it became harder with other teachers because they spoke faster. I didn't want to be caught using this method because I thought I might be made fun of by the other students.

Once I stopped this method of "reading lips", I was lost once again, now in high school. I tried using "looking into the teacher's eyes method" and it still created complications for me. I attempted to write down what is being said, as making this a visual. This worked for two reasons, if it went over my head I discovered I still had it written down to go back to and go over it. I was now using my hearing and the words on paper since were a visual. When it didn't work, it was only because the teacher spoke faster (I discovered) than what I can write down, I would be lost and would put my pencil down and just sat there pissed off yet, I had refused to return to reading lips. I was in early years of high school when I figured it out. I was used to looking into another's one eye only where I was able to remove this blurriness and still have a focus point. I found that I could remain focused but now I had some other issues that became exposed.

I would need to look away at times because I could easily lose my thought or become incapable of expressing what it was I was just speaking about. What I began doing was looking away briefly and I could then see within a visual "video like goings on within" and or could also spot a pause moment in the video and capturing "like a picture and I would describe this picture" or video that just played about getting my thoughts out or the point across with communicating with another human being. Here it was finally! I was using the very methods I would use while with God or Jesus. One point, what was so simple and never a thought to present for one to focus while using one's eyes need be a focus point and with looking into another's one eye produces this very thing!

At this point I was reaching out more with my discoveries to another referring to my issues with learning. While in middle school I shared with my councilor some of my discoveries I learned so far I having issues with learning. Distractions while in the classroom. One solution I came up with to try after she mentioned I try sitting in the front of the classroom and maybe this might remove some of these distractions I was experiencing. I thought this was a great idea; however, I visualized where I felt best I sit, and picked to the right side from the middle center, front second row from the door. This helped, some. (Why I didn't pick that furthest seat was I remembered my peer that came up behind me while standing in line that day and found it calmed me. Having another near would be to my right side stopped other distractions from entering. Such as the door leading out to the hallway, etc...)

Chapter 8

I share more about my school years, (briefly)

I was learning, but at a slower pace, picking up a little here and there. I shared some personal experiences that had brought about self-discoveries. I sought and came up with the solutions that helped me to grow with learning. Whatever the reason, be it I was born this way (where I needed an introduction as to how it is one processes (etc...) or it stemmed from my early trauma). I think it was more so the first instance and the trauma only increased my anxiety. I don't believe it created it. When I look on my first memory, it reveals that I caught process and usage of other areas that one grows with learning and using those processes to produce speech needed come into play. I grasped "process" which came about naturally (automatically) at the common proper age where I did eventually speak. However, I didn't hear more about this process with learning or discovering how I processed to learn and retain after entering school. It wasn't coming about naturally (automatically) like speech did and while I was in a school environment, I needed much more input.

I remained in the dark with my focus stuck upon this serious issue hindering me and was getting in the way. This issue was possibly affecting this natural (automatic) occurrence that was to come about. Personally, I don't believe that was the case, rather once entering school I was exposed more so, I had learning complications in the way of learning by traditional methods that are used to teach. My biggest issue was that I needed the knowledge!

I recall that I began spotting I was doing much better at home with my friendships and using my eyes and speech and hearing. I would analyze this before God during bedtime for sometime; in how could these examples through my friendships at home help me to carry them over while in school. This is what eventually helped me with moving past my awkwardness with my peers. Gradually, over time, (this issue with my peers at school) I conquered some of these in middle school. Looking back, it would appear since I was shy, but wasn't most times, I just was lost, confused and incapable of speaking my thoughts (or having no thought flowing) and my voice working together at the same time were difficult mostly in this environment.

Back then they had Study Skills classes and this was the only extra help available to me. They never could figure me out; they needed to help me and I knew I had to teach myself how to learn. Jesus didn't speak on any of these issues, but I learned early on and trusted He would present clues for me to spot. He did and I spotted the issues causing my awkward feelings and knew it was up to me to try and fix this, meaning I was capable of spotting these clues. I found that fixing these issues is what I had taken from Jesus not speaking or else I believed He would speak, like when He spoke that first time and gave me my favorite number. I believed Jesus felt I could figure this out for myself during those years.

I did wish to learn more about Jesus in His journey on earth in my later grammar school years I believe. I did watch a movie about Jesus' life and where I had taken in what Jesus experienced, as well as I had learned in this same way, of Moses journey on earth. My dad had these movies on our screen when they came around again each year. This is how I best learned, unbeknownst to me. During religious class time, I mentioned I had much difficulty learning or for that matter retaining, if I picked up something. This pathway is visual and this I easily could connect with. I was not figuring out that I am a visual learner at this time. Fast forwarding a few years; at the end of 10th grade of high school, I was offered to take English class in films. I was failing English and risked not graduating. The counselor at the school thought this could work and was correct. I almost was exempt from the final exam due to the fact that I was passing in high grades on tests relating to movies I had seen. I still wasn't connecting that I was a visual learner. Only later in years through my counselor, it had been brought to my attention.

I was now finished with my school years, but I have more to add outside of these school years.

Chapter 9

An intervention from God and Jesus possibly was through an angel

I wish to share some other personal experiences had with Jesus and God and this continues through the rest of the chapters.

I am now past the resolved initial occurrence of my early trauma and I had continued in keeping things of the same, being this was basically all I now knew. Up until then with both God and Jesus, I though, at one point I became aware that I was a little different from my new close friends. I was establishing at home regarding my personal relationship I had with both God and Jesus. With my new friendships at home, I did better with engaging socially than with peers through school although this had improved, as well.

I am returning to my younger years outside of a learning environment. I had two close friends through my neighborhood, established when I was around eight or nine years of age. My two new friends and I learned early on that they didn't attend a church like I was going to every Sunday. Eventually, I discovered they didn't talk with Jesus or God like I do. Through them, it opened another learning experience for me where overtime I wanted and felt the need to put into words explaining what I experienced with Jesus and God. I came up with "I get the voice and visions" from them. At this time, I was experiencing not just hearing their voice but, had begun receiving visions.

The voice is self-explanatory. This is when they speak verbally. This is the one I have discussed often so far. The visuals (in a visual form, either a picture or more so as like a video playing within my head) had also become at times, received of something forth coming to pass, so that is where I came up with this term visions. Each one I got did come to pass, be it at that moment or a day or 6 months to some years ahead. Once again I turned to this movie "King of Kings" much later in my years and discovered my answer. It was a means of receiving through them both the voice (most times) and visions and it was through the Holy Spirit.

The sign of the cross goes "In the name of the Father (God) and the son (Jesus) and of the Holy Spirit"! Another important detail I recalled was when Jesus mentioned to the Disciples that God will send the Holy Spirit upon them and for them to not be afraid once He leaves this earth, while spreading the good news of Jesus! I personally came up with "I get the voice and visions" from them and had seen these as gifts. Over time I was learning that those close to me didn't experience this and I felt this need should be there. Be it a need to share my personal relationship with them to another person (if either spoken on behalf for this other's sake) I can share "I get the voice and visions" from them. Over time, I received the voice not only for myself but this came in handy at least to explain to another.

Also, what was difficult was including another now from up in heaven into this small tight circle bond relationship I had now established. This is a good time to share how for years outside of God and Jesus being my center world, I heard of Angels and Guardian Angels as I was growing, I had learned some about the Disciples, the Saints and also the Blessed Mary however, I just wasn't getting it because I still remained centered upon God and Jesus for many years to come. Being this relationship was formed due to unique circumstances so early into my young life that it had made it difficult for me in becoming basically open with grasping anything within my reasoning. However, back then when I was expanding other friendships (those I just mentioned) outside of God and Jesus, a close-knit circle was being established. (This has been a slow process getting.)

Much later in my years, I started hearing about angels. I can only think of two possible occasions where my guardian angel would be. The first time, I was age twelve and wasn't speaking with Jesus in this moment, although I believed at first it was Jesus when I felt a presence near. I recognized this intervention was kind of different from an encounter than how I was accustomed to, which sort of baffled me following it. This was an intervention I never encountered before through Jesus and God. I believe it was Jesus and also may have been my guardian angel's presence.

My first time, I was with my two young girlfriends. One was ten and the other eleven. I was twelve at this time. We were hanging out at the school grounds near where we lived. There was an incline off the pavement path with trees and it was somewhat as like a hill, having tall grass, which was the enticing factor. One of my two friends mentioned rolling down this hill. My instincts kicking in, I felt this was not a smart thing to do. I had seen some trash, like pieces of paper type debris. However, despite what I thought, it wasn't a smart idea and I shared this with them. They thought I was being overly cautious and that I was only thinking of being practical. I gave in to my better judgment and did it once, rolling slowly and stopping halfway down this hill.

All three of us gathered back at the top and I felt a presence coming near, believing it to be Jesus, I went instantly on pause mode, so to speak, as I normally did and waited to hear what is told to me this time. As this presence grew nearer than of the norm, I quickly asked God if I am safe, although He didn't answer, I still felt I was safe because God was aware and was near. Once this male placed his hands on my shoulder, thinking was at first Jesus, I froze waiting to hear what will be said to me. This was the first and only time I was not only touched on the shoulder (top right shoulder) by a male hand but, felt his face close to mine believing at first it was Jesus. It could have been Him or it could have been my guardian angel stopping me from what I was about to go and do, which was rolling down this hill a second time. Although I thought I recognized Jesus' voice as I was told, "Do not roll down the hill there is broken glass," all the while His hand remaining on my shoulder. I was more focused on His hand on my shoulder than picking up if this voice was of the same, though I listened and I began to speak to my two friends. They were already aware that Jesus talks to me at this time and God and they might recall some that was spoken I had forgotten but that did come to pass. He removed His hand and I felt His presence leaving. To me for Jesus to intervene in this way I believed during these precious moments was on our behalves following what was told me, yet I won't lie, I did breathe easier once he removed his hand off my shoulder and distance occurred.

I was not certain how they would handle that I had told them Jesus had just spoken to me. Instead, I said I am not doing this because there is broken glass and they were about to go ahead and do it anyway. I told them they shouldn't but they disregarded me and went for it. I felt dread coming. Sure enough, one of my friends made it somewhere down the hill and let out a loud piercing scream (she was the ten year old). A metal broken soda can cut her into the knee cap area badly. Her mother was alerted and brought her to the hospital and was tended to.

I became very protective over my two friends at this very moment and would share a couple days later that Jesus came and this time touched my shoulder while He warned me. I did take this unique intervention as a blessing and knew that there were lessons I should take from it, my friend got hurt really badly. For starters, had I trusted and listened to my intuition. If I would have never rolled down the hill the first time it might have been more convincing for them not to do it.

Following this intervention, it made me become even more observant and cautious not only for my own self but for others. I became aware that I was to listen to my intuition, as Jesus stepped in to intervene, not only for my sake but also for how my two friends behaved. I gained a reputation of being like the mother hen. I was the cautious one amongst my friends. Oh well, that didn't bother me any!

I had many similar interventions, minus my shoulder being touched for not only me but for others. Mostly, it was for children's sake that might be in harm's way. One form was that I would feel Jesus' presence first then hear "car". This meant a car was approaching and a child or children were in harm's way either riding their bike or running around and not spotting the car in time and the driver wouldn't see them quickly enough. I had grown since this experience and I know there is a difference between me being observant and cautious. I knew where I was utilizing common sense and intuition means, and this also worked not only for me but for others like when Jesus would come close and speak, like "car". Then as time gone by, while our neighborhood kids were out and about including my own child, all I needed to hear was "car".

This presence of a male, who touched my shoulder on this one occasion, I mentioned could have come through an angel, or was it my guardian angel? Back then, I was not familiar with angels and guardian angels and wasn't for many years to come. I might have heard of them but didn't associate having a connection, so to speak. I heard very little about them, but I did not understand that God or Jesus could be also working through an angel back then for me. I mentioned earlier that I was a real slow learner referring to my religious education. I was aware that Arch Angel Gabriel spoke with Jesus and much later became aware that he is known as the Arch Angel that speaks with us on earth and it might have been him. However, this was also my first exposure to this very possibility that others sent from God might intervene. Once again I never shared this with my mom and had I done so, she might have brought up back then an angel. I recalled thinking back on it for sometime to come and went over it in my head, being this intervention was different outside of Jesus' hand placed on my shoulder. Even this was a first for me, as well as experiencing that the voice sounded as if it was coming from sort of close outside my right ear. I also felt his face near mine, yet only heard from within and it was not a whisper but was of a deep male voice, as best I can describe it. (Meaning; my two friends very close by couldn't and didn't hear him speak).

The second time occurred when I was in my late teens and it might have been either my guardian angel or an Arch Angel. The voice I heard seemed somewhat different and more words were used I noticed. One happened later in my teens and I was at a convenience store. I was running late and I was going to buy a baby gift for my friend and was looking for a baby plaque. I came across a "Footprints" plaque. I felt a presence coming near me, at first thinking it was Jesus. I waited and heard, "Give her this (Footprints). She will need this. There is something wrong with the baby, but the baby will be OK". I felt, "How can I explain why I am giving this to her?" I felt this was not a baby shower type gift. I grabbed a baby plaque instead and went and stood in a long line. I was running late to her baby shower as it was. While in line, I just was having difficulty with this because of what I was told and I was torn. I was not sure (as in the past) this was Jesus on this specific encounter, but felt it was from God, like a messenger or an angel. I was spoken to a second time and it was by the same messenger or angel. His presence I never felt. It left me wondering, "How will I feel if I don't listen when this comes to pass?" Well, this statement settled it. I got out of the line and went back and grabbed the plaque "Footprints" and stood again at the end of the growing longer line.

At this point, I was feeling apprehensive, like I was feeling that now I was this messenger of bad news "forth coming type of deal", but good news is in the end and he will be OK. Well, I handed her my gift and said not one word. I already knew this was an odd baby gift. I was not about to share any of what was spoken, at least not at this time. Shortly following his birth it was discovered that he needed open-heart surgery immediately. The positive good news was that now I trusted what I had been told and that the baby would be OK. All of what had been spoken about this handpicked gift through God did come to pass. He did survive his surgery, thankfully, and I was glad I did listen in the end.

Chapter 10

My stupid moment during the start of my Adolescent years

I am returning to another encounter though it was private between Jesus and me.

This was my stupid moment during me entering into my adolescent years. I felt at odds at this point because Jesus was Jesus but he also still was like a parent figure. I spoke with Him on this issue where I felt I am not getting to experience like others when they are away from their parents. I so regretted later that all these years had past when I asked Him back at around age thirteen or fourteen to give me some space, so to speak as being a parent figure. I believed it was I who projected this in my mind. I felt His presence and I witnessed a sort of curtain going over Him. This one time, I felt I saw Him up in the sky and as I shared I won't forget Him and still will believe in Him, yet this curtain went up as I watched. I had a thought that I might not hear from Him since I panicked. I asked Jesus, "What I will be when I grow up?" All He said was, "Designer."

The curtain was up. I went numb following it. I still talked with Him constantly and relied on the feeling of His presence still yet, I never felt this curtain come down. Through the years, Jesus began more so speaking to me through visions, more than Him early on talking with me at this point in my life. I still picked up His presence and little was I now being spoken to, when I spoke with Him, but during times He would speak through a vision with me instead. Although Jesus or God has spoken to me at times, these visions were from now both, God or Jesus, in how I reasoned with separating each of them. I was still connecting with each of them in a personal relationship developed early on. Example: if I am directly talking to God and received either a vision or verbal spoken to be Him giving me this, or if I am directly talking to Jesus now received either a vision or verbal spoken to be Him giving me this. Later, grown in some learning was *through* the Holy Spirit in communicating with me, in my reasoning still was of God (part with) and or of Jesus (part with) and they being the Holy Trinity (three) separate, but united. For me, my foundation was with God and Jesus and it was developed and formed so early on. I needed this to remain intact but have slowly become open to growing, taking baby steps forward and becoming open to angels, guardian angels and Arch Angels. I believe this is OK with them that I am taking baby steps forward, recalling like me thinking Jesus' last name was Christ. Over time I did grasp my error and I felt I was given grace and not a reprimand by either of them. This is somewhat in same lines. Even past as I had grown into an adult, I still needed to have this sort of relationship where I conversed with them and they with me. Even though it was not as often (let's say per a single day) as it was when I was a child where it was more constant.

Chapter 11

Double whammy my second trauma and hear from God and Jesus

Back in my late teens I had a double whammy occurrence about the same time both at my job (a co-worker) and personal life (a boyfriend) and both (separate) experiences harmed me very deeply. Unfortunately, I had experienced a second trauma. I was a mess.

New things were emerging in my relationship with both God and Jesus. They began to use other, more commonly known, methods at times to reach me to share a message I needed to hear. I realize this pathway is more commonly known where God or Jesus speaks to us at one's church (or place) of worship. Once again, I knew Jesus and God were aware, but I was very distraught in my circumstances at this point. I haven't been to church in awhile and began going again. Secretly hoping God or Jesus might speak to me, they both did! It came from God on the first time and the second time was through Jesus.

The first time was through a mass (two different times) on a Sunday and occurred months a part while mass was in session. The Priest would talk out of the blue and (on these two times) had nothing to do with the sermon at all. I instantly grasped it was for my benefit because I spotted in this message was what I needed to hear and it was pertaining exactly to some things that recently occurred in my life, which were very bad. Just following occurrences a boyfriend at that time and a lady from my job, both harmed me deeply and as a result, I experienced a double whammy, (my second trauma).

At that time, on top of me taking in somewhat literal or thinking somewhat literally, having learning disabilities and finding words to speak up or defend myself, I now fell into shock and was fighting off this deep pit of despair. I went to church. The Priest came out *during* the mass, out of the blue and said you are going through … It was exactly what had all I felt had just hit me. I left devastated that I could ever imagine that I would be going through something of the likes of this and on top of it all, my boyfriend and what all he had done to me. It had also altered my world, turning it upside down. As well I had to quit my job. It was that bad, is all that I will say. I was somewhat reassured leaving mass on that day that all will be well and it did comfort me some. I knew Jesus and God were with me as I was going through this; still I now had to get past all of this. Here, another crisis and this to me was far worse than my first. At least that is how I was taking this.

During another mass later in that year, I was told, "Do not dwell." So, I fought not to dwell. I never looked up this word to make sure I understood it, but to me I took it as "don't think about it." Sadly, much later in my years, I fell into the trap and I began dwelling. I was trying to fix this on my own instead of with a counselor (therapist) and a Priest. That was my biggest downfall. I also realized that it wasn't going to be overnight. Once again, I was in for another long haul. I continued to focus on these two messages and this helped me to move on. Later, I fell into the trap unbeknownst to me that I was "dwelling." These attacks were sort of like a flashback and they began and increasing. What a disaster these attacks had become. (I will share briefly shortly).

I still heard from God and Jesus through familiar methods. I had grown accustomed to since childhood, past my second trauma occurrences, and the two messages received while I was at church. After the first attempt to find a counselor (early on) that could help me, I had no success. I stopped looking and chose not to think about it and this helped. Eventually, (several years later) I sought out a counselor. When things began growing worse, I called my angel on earth. I was doing this on my own and I was trying to fix this alone instead of with a counselor (therapist). This proved to be my biggest downfall. You can't fix alone what you don't fully get or understand. This is why I fell further and deeper in a bad way.

I had multiple traumas occurring all at once. During that time (the ones I mentioned) and even new ones past this had occurred. By the time I found a wonderful counselor, I was already developing some serious complications and they were only appearing to grow worse. As my life was unraveling during counseling, so was my situation growing worse with having attacks (flashbacks). These issues were not resolved at this point and the attacks added panic within me and part of this was contributing to these attacks as well. Unbeknownst to me, I was "Dwelling" and this is what increased my situation. (Not in a good way).

What I was experiencing (again) is that I began having difficulty speaking inwardly to Jesus (as like in my early years) and feeling His presence nearby was becoming more difficult (though knew he was near). This was also contributing to these attacks as well.

Another piece of the puzzle I discovered later. I flip-flopped in going back and forth with the idea of "Do I have learning disabilities?" Once I had finished high school, I mostly let these thoughts go. My counselor discovered that I have learning disabilities, which opened me up to encounter some of those bad things. I had several bad things that have occurred to me over the years and she helped me through not only why I sought out a counselor, but contributed some as why of all those bad things had happened to me.

Over time, I also sought and found a spiritual guide who also was Heaven sent. He was very helpful with my spiritual crisis. I was eventually diagnosed as having Post Traumatic Stress Disorder (recovered). Post Traumatic Stress Disorder, also known as PTSD. By the time I received this diagnoses, my recovery to having this diagnoses was given to me and with recovery there was not a long period in-between (less than two years easily) outside of prior years of counseling.

Chapter 12

God sent three messages
through a close friend for me

God also exposed to me a second pathway by sending me a message on a personal level. God went through my girlfriend (I had known her now more than thirty years) to share words for me to hear from them. Through her, God answered me three different times on a personal level. Each time was during her sleep and was through her dream-state that she picked up what was from God and that it was for me. He came to her without her knowledge of what I had said or asked God each of the three times. Each time this confirmed what it was I had asked for or spoken to God about.

The first time was through means of a visual (a year past second trauma) and the other two times were verbal messages (later in years). Following my hearing her share the first time to me, I needed hearing to ease my severe anxiety. I was experiencing moving back to my home state. When she shared with me her dream from God, I instantly felt at peace, knowing this was from

God. I so much appreciated that He had made a connection to and for me through her, which brought me much comfort. All of what she had seen and heard in her dream did come to pass a couple of days later.

This one I will share. The first time she had a dream about one of the people that had caused the most severe traumas to me. I had returned to the state where I grew up and I had feared running into him. She said she had a dream that we ran into him at a public place. The encounter went unusually well. There was a peaceful feel to the meeting for her. (She had been almost as frightened as I was about me running into him). After she told me, it eased the severe anxiety. I instantly felt at peace, knowing it was from God. I so appreciated that he made a connection for me through her that brought me so much comfort. What she saw and heard in her dream came to fruition a couple of days later. We were at a friend's house, and ...., showed up. He had asked me to go for a walk to talk. If not for that dream I never would have gone, but I felt God was telling me it was going to be ok. I went, we spoke briefly, and I said the things I needed to say. We went back to the house and he left. I never saw him again.

Another time, later in years, they came to her again. This time it was about something I was asking God a question. Though I was very upset, angry, and filled with tears while presenting my question, God answered immediately that night through her (again coming to her while she slept) I would have an answer. This is personal and will remain a private matter in what I asked and was told to her for me. She told me my answer, and I asked her who she was speaking with. She also talked with God about what was mentioned to her and she said it was God.

One last time to date, God went through her through using this same method was while she slept. I asked Him another question, referring to something I was working very hard on, (book about my son), although this answer was given to her to pass on to me. It has not come to pass as of yet, but I trust it will also come to pass.

Chapter 13

I was in severe crisis and Jesus did come to my aid

God or Jesus has spoken to me quite easily from time to time. If they chose to, more so was on a personal level, even past these times when attending church and at times while I was in severe crisis (second trauma), but appeared not when it was during the worst time that lasted three weeks that I could pick up (looking back, I spot they were). One example was through a verbal message and it was for my son in his younger years, many times I would hear Jesus speak, "Go, check on your son." Sure enough, he was about to get into mischief or was in harm's way.

Another unique intervention was in a supermarket during those three weeks being of the worst episodes. I had had anxiety and panic attacks in the past. However, this time was one of the worst I had ever encountered. I was in a bad way and I had asked Jesus for His intervention ASAP, knowing He was fully aware of all that I was experiencing in this moment, yet knew not how He could help me quickly! A man stopped in prayer (his hands in prayer).

In front of him was his cart with some food and as I turned the corner, I spotted him. As I neared him and walked past him, my severe anxiety and panic attack seized. My first thought when I passed him was that this was a man that happened to be very spiritual and close to God. Later, I also thought he could have been an angel. All I can say is how gratefully thankful I was, whoever he was. I was very grateful to Jesus and God for their intervention, working through another they had shown now to me.

At times over the years after these several weeks had passed, though not every Sunday, I would watch through my TV a mass and sometimes I would still hear from either of them through this pathway. Since the time I recovered from PTSD, I also have heard from them directly although still it wasn't as frequently as when I was a child.

Chapter 14

Sharing two other times Jesus spoke to me

I wish to briefly mention about another time Jesus spoke to me. Following being counseled for some time, at this point her husband's health had grown bad all of a sudden. I talked with Jesus and was upset, not only for them but I needed her. I respected that her husband comes first of course. Jesus told me, "He will have a kidney transplant." Then I shared this with her on her answering machine and for the next week, while he was getting tested, the doctors discovered it was his kidney and said he needs a kidney transplant. She called me up and left a message on my answering machine sharing that the prediction (what I was told) was correct. She was his donor. After eleven years of a successful transplant sadly, he died of other medical issues and is greatly missed by his wife and children and grandbabies, loved ones and friends. Although I didn't know him personally, this broke my heart hearing of the news of his passing.

Years have passed since I had a full recovery from PTSD. This one time Jesus spoke to me directly and I will share it. I got laid-off from work due to the recession and (although thankful) I found a job in a retail store. At times, I was working in the stockroom and my salary greatly decreased. I would get frustrated from all of these conditions and I had other dreams I wanted to pursue, yet felt they might never occur now that I was experiencing money issues big time. At my age, I now began focusing on my finances (I was aging). This one time, I was frustrated (working in stockroom) and I was talking with Jesus. I felt not only am I stuck, due to my circumstances and was doing this form of work while I am aging but it was becoming an issue for me. I heard Him speak as I was walking into work, "Age is just a number." Amen! So often I return to this message, as I proceed forward, which helps me in getting through work and I move forward not dwelling on my age. Guess what, this works!

Chapter 15

My uncertainty over visions

I was given a vision, though I had a doubt at that moment that I might have come through myself.

It was when I was living in Florida and a close friend was leaving the island on his motorcycle. I was very concerned and received a vision. He would be turning right off the island and in my car would be making a left. His motorcycle was not running well, however, after asking him more than once to let me follow him at least to a main road, he firmly said no and that he would be fine (very stubborn). After he turned right, as I was turning left, I got a vision from Jesus. In this vision, he was broken down just after an overpass over water (canal), which was a couple of yards away from the spot where he was turning right. Due to my doubt if it was I or from Jesus, I was sharing to Jesus he was being a butt head, stubborn. I was pissed he was so stubborn in this moment and I continued home. The next day, I called to see how he faired and yes, he did breakdown where the vision had shown.

Well, this removed any doubts and I was convinced that this was a vision from Jesus. I shared that Jesus told me and I also shared he was being so stubborn. I was pissed at him at that time because he wouldn't allow me to follow him to a main road. I did feel bad and regretted that I didn't turn around, at least to check that spot. I have had other times where Jesus or God has spoken on behalf of another, though this is all I will share.

Another time some years past, this time was through Jesus spoken method; again I had a doubt at that moment that it might have come through me. The reason for my confusion was that I suddenly became anxious over the upcoming birth of my close friends first baby and didn't understand why. I was running late getting to work, and was driving there. I was in thought with Jesus about this very thing. I heard call her the baby is in trouble; something has gone wrong for this baby girl. Sadly I didn't listen, believing this time it was me and my anxiety for her upcoming delivery. I found out later even if I called her at that moment, saving this baby girl was not to be. The umbilical cord was wrapped tightly around her leg which caused her passing. I was devastated for this baby and her parents and loved ones. Many times I went over these moments in my head, and eventually understood that Jesus was coming for this little baby girl. To this day this little angel Valerie remains in my heart and thoughts, knowing she is living up in heaven along with her younger brother or sister, Sam or Kate, (called Sam/Kate) and each remains a part in their family's life always. I added Valerie's picture in here.

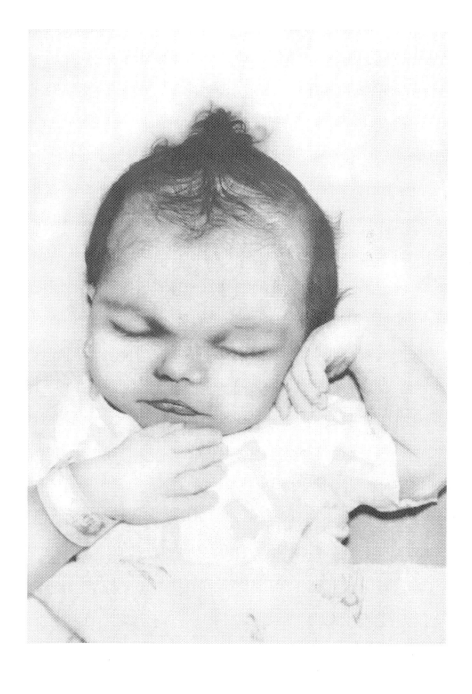

Chapter 16

I become open to asking others for prayers

When I became open to getting to know some others while here on earth, those whom were close to Jesus during his journey on earth, although I do acknowledge the many.

These some are the Blessed Mary, St. Ann (the mother to Mary), St. Joseph (Mary's Spouse), and St. Jude and my latest I am opening up to are my guardian angel. I personally began acknowledging and including the Blessed Mary, the Saints, Angels, and my guardian angel (I was once unaware I had) into my life, however, I was not open to forming a relationship with anyone else other than God and Jesus for many years (was past high school). When I came to seeing it this way (later years) is what opened me up to turning to Mary, (I personally acknowledge her and call her Blessed Mary, as some in the Christian faith do) was the first person.

Jesus said prior to taking his last breath, spoken to John standing before him, "Behold, your mother." She was also still present before Jesus, near John. I have turned to her twice since high school (share shortly). Through her prayers has also shown me that I received God's protection, though I didn't return to her again until later in my years. I returned to God and Jesus only as was my usual norm. I had no further need was how I felt at that time.

Years later, I did turn to her again. I had a need, as well as, I personally wanted to get to know her while here on earth. I recalled again what Jesus had spoken near his last breath (including her so to speak, in my daily life) and that was my personal choice in me wanting to do it. I didn't experience her presence or hear her talking to me directly, but I knew she heard and was praying for me in my recovery (my second trauma). I also found comfort through the Holy Rosary and the Blessed Mary when I was experiencing many attacks (flashbacks).

I also discovered in reciting the Holy Rosary within (as also being a prayer) that a solution to these attacks (flashbacks) I was experiencing would help me with fighting these attacks within, this helped tremendously over time towards my full recovery. As I was growing comfortable with coming open to including others up in heaven (those some mentioned) into my daily life, this was also when I associated it as of the same as me asking another here for prayers. This made me comfortable by including them above as well.

Following reading a prayer I discovered that it was also making me at ease when it comes down to them praying for me and those that I had mentioned. I heard many times, another would ask another, to keep me or a loved one who was not well, in your prayers. This is a beautiful thing and I have been doing this, as well with others, prayers are heard, prayers are powerful and this I learned through others here.

Despite knowing I could go to God or Jesus directly and do, I still turn to another (here) asking for prayers. Today it is heard also through this way. For me, in how I see this and how I reason this is my personal choice for wanting to form a personal relationship with (some mentioned) and if another doesn't see it how I see it now, this is OK and I respect it. I didn't see it in my early life. I didn't understand it the way I do now and I wasn't reprimanded due to this. Through them it exposed to me this invitation to including them into my daily life. Respecting another Christian's belief was told to me by Jesus (share in chapter 17). If someone wants to read these prayers of the Saints, or Holy Rosary, then by all means, either look them up or talk with a priest to guide you in getting to these to read for yourself. I have friends of different faiths and also in the Christian Faith community and respect all the different faiths. I am not pushing my self-discoveries on to anyone. That is not my intention with this book I will be sharing. I only am sharing what I have personally experienced through my journey with both God and also Jesus and including becoming open minded to including others up in heaven that were close to Jesus while He was here on earth. I see it as I am asking for prayers through them.

I also acknowledge Abraham (the first person God spoken to directly) and Moses. I acknowledge all of the Old Testament, though I only learned (mentioned) so much through watching Moses' movie early years and some through Bible Study. I acknowledge also all the Disciples and in their closeness to both God and Jesus and the paths they were called to. Including Abraham, like Moses, etc... Through them all, I found personally it also contributed to bringing me closer to knowing what is pleasing to God, also through Jesus' guidance in seeing this. As I mentioned, for many years, my focus was with them helping me here on a personal level and I still do this for myself. If I am wrong about something be it on a personal level or religious way, they will show me.

I have three special moments and share these, one is bittersweet

This is the first time I had turned to the Blessed Mary. I did on one occasion in my past (late teens out of high school) pray the Holy Rosary one time. It was when I was in a trapped situation and thankfully by the time I finished, the phone rang and help arrived shortly after. I lived in a basement apartment in a private home and only received incoming phone calls. I heard someone in the backyard and the backdoor was my only escape. The timing of the phone ringing, just as I had finished praying, I personally don't believe that was a coincidence, but a blessing I received from God through the Blessed Mary's prayers. Only I didn't get it, was this message OK to turn to her to also ask for her prayers, until much later in life.

I am sharing something that pertains to my first experience coming from Jesus as well God, through a Saint, was this Saint Joseph Prayer. In my later years around 29, referring to my religious education, although I was being raised in the Catholic faith, I was not growing through this form of teaching in my young years as I mentioned. This comes about of some of it much later in my years.

At this time, I have now grown accustomed to another asking of another for prayers. I began doing this and it is what opened me to those that called on Saints. It was of asking them for prayers as well (mentioned). During my first exposure from

Jesus through a Saint, I experienced and was inspired through my dad, who always prayed this prayer. He prayed the Saint Joseph prayer (and you receive protection if prayed faithfully everyday and at the same time). I decided after my dad mentioned I should be doing this, I did. After first reading of the words in this prayer, I personally didn't feel it threatened my personal relationship with both God and Jesus in any way at this time (as how I felt first reading of the Holy Rosary) and became open to turning to him for his prayers. I had been praying this prayer for a while. "Well", a Hurricane (I believe it was Hurricane Andrew in 1991 or 1992) and it was fixing to hit Port Charlotte, Florida and also would hit Boca Raton, Florida. "Guess what?" My dad, mom and aunt were visiting in Boca Raton with my aunt's relative and I was visiting in Port Charlotte Florida while this hurricane was about to arrive and hit land. I was the one with the car and staying with close friends (she and her two daughters) were her home and refused to drive further inland (her home was close to canals leading to the gulf not far off, about 10 minutes away).

We were listening to the broadcasting of this hurricane on TV. I continued to encourage her for us all leaving but with no luck. I was a nervous wreck (literally) and I wouldn't leave them. I found an electrical outlet. I saw her iron and clothing in need of ironing and began to iron. Moments later, the announcer just told everyone to stay put. The hurricane will hit within five minutes. I was frantic and inwardly speaking with Jesus and felt His presence, then with God felt His presence, then back with Jesus, then with God and felt both presences each time. This is how it went (mentioned, I always separated them) while with God and this Saint Joseph prayer I had been praying popped into my thoughts then I felt Jesus' presence.

I recalled in this prayer promise, I will be protected and so will my dad and those in Boca Raton. I instantly felt peace. I didn't feel the hurricane would harm us, yet I still thought it would come. "Guess what?" The hurricane never came nor did it hit Boca Raton. How I had first taken it was this hurricane had never hit land. I was gratefully in shock at this awesome experience. Also, a self-discovery was made. It was God, as well as Jesus that had a part of this pop up and was this Saint Joseph prayer I prayed that had shown *me* personally I was OK in praying this prayer? Also was confirming to *me* of the other Saint's prayers? Did I get through the Saint Joseph's prayer to have received God's protection? Later in that day, I heard sadly that this hurricane did hit land and it made a turn within this five- minute window and hit Venus harder than was forecasted. For me of that day turned out to be a bittersweet moment!

I will mention the second time shortly of when I turned to the Blessed Mary. Other times Jesus or God had spoken and it was for protection purposes. For example, not only for myself, but also for others like "car" which meant a car is coming and either it was my own child or another child or children were in harm's way. (Mentioned) I was always in communication with Him and God and eventually I was given visions in my late teen years. Each vision I received did come to pass except one, a thought popped into my mind, I had prayed ten Hail Mary's and although it did come about, no harm followed. Thanks be to God and Jesus and Blessed Mary's intervention of prayers over him.

This vision was about my oldest cousin and how he was going to get into an accident on a bridge that night. It was snowing at the time and despite the bad weather conditions, he still chose to risk the drive and left. Unbeknownst to him is what I was told about him. Though overheard, he was asked not to leave due to the bad weather, but still left. On the bridge he did experience having issues driving over this bridge and I mentioned this very thing to his mom once he had made it safely to his destination. Thankfully, he didn't get into an accident and made it safely to his destination. I believe it was through the Blessed Mary's intervention and her prayers for him.

Chapter 17

I was answered by God and Jesus through Mass

When I returned to church later in years, these times were answered to me over different things.

I began to understand what was occurring in my life prior to church that week or dealing with religious questions I was having and also while I was having a random thought over something and why didn't take it to them? I still received confirmation. I was heard and was answered during church. I began sharing these with my Spirit Guide eventually and I also mentioned these to my counselor (therapist). I was very grateful for them reaching out to me during those times and looking back I spotted their efforts while I was in the mist of the worst moments of my life. God and Jesus were still determined to let me know they were so ever near. I have heard from them during these past several years in a direct way, though not as frequent as when I was a child.

Some I will share spoken through church. Once was when I received sort of a reprimand from God. I heard again from Him past this time using this pathway, which only confirms what I knew already and where I was forgiven. Knowingly God, is Mercy, God is Love!

I already shared how I looked upon God as more like a Father, so to speak, although always knew He was God the creator from a very young child. I vented while angry to God over something I was directing towards Him and I was fully aware that He was listening. I knew later that I would hear from Him when I went to church that coming Sunday despite my apology. "Yep, I did, loud and clear"! I was not a happy camper, so to speak, and was frustrated, discouraged, and became angry. I had told God I was going to burn some of my papers and be done with them. I was working on but I didn't see any positive results of these going anywhere at that time. His reply was while church was already in session. The Priest had spoken out of the blue, but this time in a stern delivery said, "You were given gifts, you best be using them." This message had nothing to do with the sermon obviously (most messages relayed to me went). I caught this reprimand that was for my behalf and no I didn't burn the papers.

I share that some other times receiving a message through the church pathway occurring the same way, though a Priest had never spoken as sternly in a message as that one time I just mentioned.

Later in years (mentioned), when I had a counselor and a priest, as my Spirit Guide, both were my angels, as I like to call them. I was sharing with this priest all of it, (who already had become my spirit guide), and he said I should write it down. I chose not to and did feel I needed to stop going for a while because I felt

I could easily fall into creating something in the week prior to Sunday Mass and this is not what I felt I ever would want to do! I did write down ones I could recall, including prior and past these times. Some things I did ask of God or Jesus during the week that I was in search of how to understand, prior to attending church. I asked Jesus how I would describe how I was brought up to another person. Later that week, I attended Sunday Mass and the priest brought up during his moments of talking with us and mentioned "you" (as referring to all) are being raised by the spirit world! Hearing this made perfect sense, as well validated what I asked him earlier in the week. Yes, Jesus and God began speaking to me through Mass in session, coming through a priest in my later years more so when they chose to speak.

Another Sunday, during the week I was speaking with Jesus and asked Him in my confusion, "How is it that there were so many different named religions alone in the Christian faith?" I found this confusing. On the following Sunday, (the same way as the other times) the priest spoke about this very subject. "How Jesus, as being the tree trunk and the branches are of the different Christian faiths of this one tree, and that all that are for him are not against him." This alleviated my confusion instantly. Another question I raised up to Jesus, although fully aware of this was, "Thou shall not kill" commandment, (war is war I get, and this I didn't bring into my question). I questioned, "But, what of self-defense for our child?" During this week, I heard another speak on TV on this very thing. It raised my question, "Would this be a sin?" Sure enough, I was answered Sunday during church in session. The priest mentioned this very thing. He spoke and used an example, "If someone broke into your home and was about to do bodily harm, let's say to your child, you're in the right to do whatever you must do to protect your child." He went on to say,

"Your child is a gift from God and it is your obligation to tend and care for this child, as well protect, even if it came down to taking another's life for protecting your child from grave harm." There were some more things I had heard messages from them up to last time I attended church, following the Scriptures read back then.

This one time I asked for a miracle (recent times), basically. This refers to my teeth. I finally went to a dentist over one tooth chipped and was informed following a full exam, was informed I needed massive work done, as well told of two teeth needing being pulled. I was very upset and spoke of this to Jesus even asking him to heal my teeth, especially of those two needing be pulled. Sunday of that week, I turned on the mass and had hoped to hear from him about my serious circumstance now in. The mass was already in session, the Priest began to say, "You're to take care of your teeth". I got my answer, no miracle was forth coming, and as well what I need be doing, got it loud and clear.

A second time occurred where Jesus touched my shoulder, was nearing the end of writing of this book, though adding it here instead.

Another first, I will share. I was awakened to hear mass on a Sunday morning, though wanted to remain in bed to sleep in. Only this time (literally) felt Jesus nudge for me to get up to hear the sermon (a first). My eyes still closed I felt his presence come closer and next felt a hand touching my blanket reaching to my shoulder underneath it. I instantly opened my eyes (had hope, though knowingly I won't see him, I didn't), is when his hand lifted off my shoulder through the blanket, and where his hand once felt lift up, I seen the blanket (as would of finger print moving away) shifted as would accordingly following. I didn't freak out, but felt the urgency of something that will be spoken I needed hear from this mass. Yes, I turned on my TV immediately; the mass already in session, oddly was past the readings and was while a Priest was speaking to us. He began saying, "Jesus didn't come to abolish the Old Testament but only to fulfill it"! After hearing this powerful message confirmed for me my acknowledgment of Abraham, Moses, and the Old Testament. The Ten Commandments, I learned of Jesus' mentions of the first two, I caught during my earlier years if one follows the first two you are honoring the rest of the eight left remaining.

Chapter 18

Heartbreaking Visions

I received very sad news and was for another which will be passing in the near future.

This is the first vision I received about someone else would be leaving us here. It was during the same year as my second trauma (much earlier in my years). I was working and a friend walked into the store and I will call him Joe. As he headed towards the back of the 7-Eleven to get a beverage, I heard Jesus tell me, "I won't see him again." I instantly became alarmed and when he came up to the register, I asked him, "What are you doing tonight?" He said he and another friend were driving a moving truck to Florida. I spoke slowly and my voice held great concern as I looked into his eyes said to him, "Please drive carefully." He nodded yes, but I didn't see in his expression the seriousness in how I meant what I said. Sadly, he got into an accident and passed. That was a difficult time for me to get past. He is very much missed by his family, loved ones and friends. This was the first time I was being forewarned about what was going to happen. I had a total of 6 times through the years, each of these affected me deeply and only

I am sharing the first three. Near to the last one I asked Jesus and God to take this from me, of knowing and they did.

This is my second vision I received about someone else. That was picture form was from God. This came about not long after the first. A distant loved one would be leaving here soon. I didn't know how this was to come about. My family and I were moving back to our home state I asked my dad if we can stop at a relative's home whom we haven't seen in a real long while due to this long distance. He said we need to keep driving or else we will hit our city late in evening which he was determined to avoid. I was upset while talking with God, saying we won't get another chance stopping to visit them, and one might no longer be here if ever we visit at a later date. I did not expect to be answered. All a sudden pictures of this family from the head (Father) down went through my thoughts and landed on the last one, the youngest, and remained longer on her picture. I caught she will be leaving, but wasn't told why, nor did I ask or thinking would be told. I felt a sense of doom and great loss come over me and became very upset by this forth coming news. I didn't share it with anyone, I had hoped maybe this outcome I just heard from God might change. Sadly Within that year, I think was six months past, we got the call this youngest daughter was in a car accident and was pronounced brain-dead, she did pass away. Back then wearing seatbelts was not common as is it today. After hearing this horrific news I still fell into shock, and was shown this did come to pass what God told me earlier. This was my second forth coming of sad news shown in a different way from the first one leaving us, I just shared with you. I caught life is so precious and we never know when our time ends here on earth and begins up there. My thoughts and prayers remained on her family over this horrific loss of their daughter and sister, girlfriend and friends near and dear to her. Over her passing, I also felt another loss I didn't get a chance to get to know her as brief as it would have been as a young adult. I questioned myself, had I shared what I was told to my dad, might we had stopped there? I never shared with my dad any of my private journeys having with God and Jesus. Here is when I had another twinge of conflict over my private life with God and Jesus having, unbeknown to my parents. I remained silent once again; I didn't speak and share any of it, other than shared with them that God and Jesus speak to me. I continued not to speak or share on each one I was told they be leaving us here. I knew life continues past here, because knowing God and Jesus, yet still ones passing is devastating none the less.

This was the third time I was being forewarned. My grandmother on my father's side (who in less than a week would be turning ninety-two), was spending time with us. She would be leaving to go back home to another state a day later. She was still very independent even at this age. I asked her about one of her recipes for pizza and I told her I wanted to learn how to make her dough. She and I bought the ingredients to make it that day before her leaving the next day.

We had everything on the table ready to go and I excused myself for a minute. She was already beginning to put things together for making her dough. When I returned, I became upset with her because the most important part I wanted to learn now was finished. Inwardly, I remained upset with her for a few days following, unbeknownst to her. Her birthday arrived and I heard Jesus speak. He said, "Call her, she will be leaving soon." I picked up the phone some moments later and was so glad I did! She passed shortly after her birthday. She is very much missed.

My fourth was an elderly man. That was verbal form was from God. This is all I will share on this. I did get to meet his wife as we cried together. He is much missed by his wife and his family and loved ones and friends.

My fifth or was my sixth time being forewarned, these were so close in time and I was overly distraught and can't place these two accurately as far as timeline. This was from Jesus, was a verbal. This is all I will share on this. This individual is much missed by their family, loved ones and friends.

My dad was losing weight and was diagnosed with having emphysema because he was a smoker. Following his passing, it came to me about how come he passed sooner rather than later, is still felt today. He was my fifth or was my sixth time being forewarned, was through God, was a verbal. This is all I will share on this. He is so much missed by all the family and loved ones.

Chapter 19

My dad's presence at his wake

At my dad's wake, I stood at his open coffin this first time and prayed and had intension to only pray one Hail Mary prayer. Only in this moment, I held my hands together and raised them upward and my fingers weren't folded. I was still in shock over his passing and over feeling the great loss of him being gone. I have no reason as to why I held my hands this way, instead of folded while in prayer, however, I felt a presence come forth the moment I began to pray this one Hail Mary inwardly, thinking it might be God. God', who shared something forth coming about my dad, as I had mentioned. This had devastated me upon hearing it and is why I thought at first was Him. This presence that came forth was over my dad's coffin (near his chest area had to be facing me) and placed their male hands over mine. This was the second time in my lifetime I had felt a hand. Once I felt His hands placed over mine (upside down to mine that rose upwards), I began feeling other presences from behind, nearing me, and some placed their hands on my shoulders.

My first thought was these were other family members that had already passed. While I stayed focused on praying this one Hail Mary prayer, it had taken longer in me praying it, because of this being totally unexpected. As well as a first experience with such a unique visit (never happened prior nor after), along with the other's presence touching my shoulder was offering me comfort and that is how I had taken it. I shared my experience with my long time girlfriend (mentioned) not long past this experience and she said it was my dad holding my hands. The moment she said this, I believed she was correct because those hands over mine I felt I believed were his hands.

Looking back, I wished I had prayed more Hail Mary's so I could have remained in my dad's presence longer.

Chapter 20

Jesus brought me
up to Heaven

My dad and I played something like" peek-a-boo or tag-your-it, your turn." My dad first came to me and I couldn't see him and then I go and see him and he can't see me.

As I have mentioned, I began recalling past memories of my own spiritual journey with God and Jesus. Following just having laid down in my bed and only resting my eyes still I was very much awake. Only moments passed when I turned to my personal relationship with God and Jesus. I dared to ask of them a very special favor and I was answered. I was given the gift of my request!

My sorrow over the loss of my dad who passed away three months earlier was heavy on my mind as I headed into my bedroom to lie down to sleep for the night. I remained wide-awake moments just following climbing into bed and I turned to Jesus and feeling Jesus' presence, I asked to see my dad. The next moment I found myself light body in weight but felt I was within my body, yet there was something covering parts of my visual for viewing with my own two eyes. As best, I thought to describe this while above was as if someone held binoculars over my eyes yet I was not feeling them being there.

All within, as like so calling it binoculars, was clear view to visually see, however outside of the frame of the so-called binoculars remained hidden for me to see yet there was no dark surrounding. I remained completely calm and felt safe and did believe I would get what I asked for (the next second, in the blink of an eye, literally) therefore, before my own very eyes I saw my dad walking down a clean sanded path about eight feet in width. This is what I was allowed to see. Not once did I question why I had a block of sorts over my vision to a wider view. I simply was very grateful to have been given this wonderful gift.

There before me, walking slowly, coming forward was my dad. He was to my right. I was on an angle from him, not directly in front but several feet away, as I would be to his left side. I instantly realized he could not see me, yet I was given this gift to see my dad because this is what I had asked for and I was given specifically this request to the "T" of my one request I had asked for. I instantly began taking in all that I could see and acknowledged how my dad had gained at least ten pounds since his passing. He was very sick before his death and lost so much weight. I also took in what he was wearing. I was already thinking I can't wait to share this wonderful gift and just being given in that very moment.

He was wearing a long sleeved buttoned down shirt, the color dark blue. His pants were also dark blue and his shoes were black, only saw the tips. He wore a hat colored white and this looked somewhat like a baseball cap type hat, although it had height like a chef's hat appearance. I thought how odd, wearing this odd unique hat and had a humorous but sincere thought in his favor of course, in that he must been given an honor having me as his daughter, because he and I did butt heads from time to time. He walked with a cane or a stick. This is the only thing of this wonderful experience I can't recall, this was the only thing I did not put into a must to remember when going back with intent to share. I did notice he was walking very slowly. My first thoughts were following that I was "taking in" seeing him and what he was wearing. I looked to his eyes. My dad always wore glasses and I saw him glassless, which was rare. What I spotted was as best as I could describe, while I was up there. What I came up with were familiar descriptions I could associate as to what I saw when looking into his eyes. It was appearing as if he was in awe and then I thought he might be reminiscing happy thoughts and I took from it that he was very happy up there. I saw more when looking into my dad's eyes. The closest I could come up with describing what I had only known (while up there), comes close to a newborn's first time looking into their parent's eyes. This radiant glow is pure love, awe. I looked at his eyes a few seconds longer. It was breathtaking. Then I took in everything else I could spot, not knowing how long I would still have up there. What I could see was past my dad's path to his right. There were trees lined perfectly apart from each other and they went on further in. The further in I could see, the shorter of the trunks I spotted. However, I wasn't able to see the full height of the trees nor spotted any branches because of this.

I noticed these trees also were thin. Each of the trees had been the same width and smooth, no bark to them and their coloring was tan, slightly bright like. This is hard for me to describe. It is my fault because I was unable to see the sky. I did come up with a season. They reminded me of our "fall season", how it appeared when I was there.

Following, I saw my dad and studied him and the background tree trunks of what I could see. I thought, "So, this must be purgatory." At this time, I just became open to the possibility that purgatory exists and spotted my dad. He was showing physical signs of healing (him gaining some weight).

Another thing I was picking up was in how peaceful it was in this place where I saw my dad. I glanced towards my right (my dad's left) and had a thought in wanting to describe the peacefulness I felt here. I felt no fear should a lion appear was how peaceful I personally felt in this place my dad was. I thought I had known what peacefulness felt like. But, in this precious moment, it was shown me a much greater peacefulness exists up there.

Well, I had taken in all that I could. "Where would I share when I return?" I had the thought that being God allowed me to be here and knowingly Jesus was with me, I thought, this is one chance in a lifetime. I felt I shouldn't do this yet, I did it anyway, sort of thing. I wanted to speak with my dad and I screamed as loud as I could, "Dad!" By the time I had stopped in this yell, I was already back home in my room, lying in my bed. In my return from up there, to back into my bed was that quick. I thought OK, I was correct and yelling is a "no-no" up there.

I still felt Jesus' presence in my room, my eyes open though couldn't see him. I asked, "Where is he going?" This time, I felt my journey going up. (Was of the same as the first times moments ago where I found myself light body in weight but felt I was within my body.) I missed the second where the male hands holding me from behind, held me going up had taken me at first. I also couldn't see (totally blind) and noticed that I felt my eyes were as wide as could be, yet no light came. We were going very fast and I spotted a feeling under my eye. The skin was moving up and down in a fast motion. Then, I began thinking that after taking in my physical now new condition, I wasn't panicking this whole while because I trusted in thinking it was Jesus bringing me to where I asked this time. Later I considered who could have brought me might have been an Angel or Arch Angel. I felt Jesus' presence the whole time, just like the first time up there and throughout my life thus far.

I still had access to think, this trip up and after going over my new physical condition was in. I turned to another thought explaining why this time I couldn't see and was experiencing a different way going up. What came to mind when I got to thinking why I was not allowed to see, was I might calculate how long it will take my dad to get to this destination of where he was heading. The moment I felt a twinge of feeling uncomfortable due I couldn't see was when we stopped in travel and I instantly got my eyesight back. It was as if the sameness as the first time, but now I had the capability I now recognized. These male hands remained holding me from behind this whole time while up there. The moment I could see, a large magnificent structure stood and thought this is the Arch I began hearing about. I instantly recognized the material the Arch was made of. This Arch had two sides only and a hollow center having a pass through also both sides were curved, connecting at the center top in equal widths of both of these side walls. I saw that this was the center.

I spotted the very same tree trunks and the sandy path my dad was on went through it to the other side. I couldn't see past it because of where I stood before this Arch. One of my first thoughts was that here in front of me was this same path my dad is on and here before me was the ending of this path was this magnificent structure, this Arch, taking up as much space as I was capable of seeing.

I had no doubt Jesus was taking me to this place because of what I had asked of Him. He did and all that I saw in my first time up there was here on this second time, only minus my dad. I personally acknowledged this as the Arch one passes through and stepping into Heaven's ground coming from what I had taken as purgatory, where my dad was walking. To me, this confirmed that this place my dad was in was purgatory. I previously mentioned that I had taken in all of what I could (allowed) see and that also I will share this with others about this magnificent journey on this second time from beginning to end when I get back.

My eyes remained upon the Arch for several moments. A totally amazing site is this Arch. This Arch had only two walls (duplicate in structure) with an opening in the front and back of these walls was a walk through. The ground was the same sand and continued all the way through. Now the walls were the very same tree trunks I had seen on my first time up moments earlier. Amazing! Only these tree trunks making this Arch were planted, touching the next tree trunk making this solid, like a sidewall (like poles) and no light can seep through either of the sidewalls (they were that close to each other). These two walls where they connected and met at the center at the top appeared as if they were bowed (bended to one another at the top center) is what I saw and had come up with for a description while I was up there. Years ago I attempted to paint on a rock all I saw while up there. I was not an artist back then, example: at that time getting the correct colors of the trees was not my main focus. I wanted to show that they are trees. On front cover are this Arch and my dad walking on this path. On the back cover Elizabeth also drew my dad walking on this path, she added the glasses he always wore. Up there I saw he no longer needed them.

It was magnificent to gaze upon. Then I tried to count how many tree trunks to one side (the opposite side would be of the same) that was to my right, only I couldn't see the farthest ones. Well in time, I knew I might not have and I wanted to explore with my eyes all of the other things that I could see, yet haven't. The number I was able to count looking from the side glance stopped at about fifteen but more had shown from the top and still there were more past fifteen. I turned to the height of this Arch before me and kind of got it, although I was still being held from behind where I was to this arch and it was appearing as if I was about up to the halfway point, slightly to the top of this Arch. Knowingly, I could be off on this measurement since I was not up against it and was not standing on the ground. I would say it could be eight or nine feet is what I came up with, yet could be totally incorrect and this Arch is higher.

I then let this go, feeling satisfied. I felt I had gathered as much information as I could to take back with me about this Arch. I glanced to the right for what else I could see. I saw some of the tree trunks, like when I saw my dad. They again appeared where again I was not seeing the tips and they were evenly planted away from the other, as well equal in distance apart. Then, I went back to looking at the Arch, spotted although couldn't see past the Arch, but above the Arch I could see some, though it was in the distance that I spotted something. What I was able to see was some of the sky and it appeared slightly bluer in color and in the far distance I had seen tall trees that looked familiar. What I had seen of these trees was the tippy top portion with green leaves. These leaves appeared greener, like the sky was slightly bluer and I thought the colors here were more vibrant than on earth.

I was able to take in all I could see and the next moment I was back in my bed. I felt my body appeared heavy and I refused to wig out. I didn't get brought back the same way as I went this second time. It was the same as the first time, in a split moment. I lay there for a while adjusting within my body and focusing on all what Jesus shown me, still in awe. Crazy as this sounds, the thought to thank Jesus as well as God, never occurred to me or this I don't recall if I said to them while falling asleep, however did just do this now, just in case I forgot.

What else? Looking back, something which didn't come to me on this second time until now, is maybe feeling Jesus' hands (or was an Angel or Arch Angel holding me, though still felt Jesus' presence) around my waist was also for my sake a reminder not to yell a second time while up there, however no one else I was blessed to see this time had shown up. Although, I did get the message on the first time once brought back and the reprimand being I was brought up a different way this second time, I wouldn't attempt to speak, nor yell on that second time visit no matter what!

I was speaking to Jesus and feeling His presence near and believed at that time it was He who brought me up to Heaven twice (yet although I still felt Jesus' presence on both times near me. The one that actually brought me could have been an Angel or Arch Angel on the second time). Still, there were two different ways I was shown. On the second time, going up to Heaven, were male hands from behind holding my waist going up and remained holding me while I was up there!

Gratefully, I was not shown, "Hell."

Thank you for participating in my journey!

Addendum

My mom read my book, she shared she was happy I finally shared all this with her.

Around the age of thirteen or fourteen I asked Jesus what I will be when I grow up and all he said was "Designer". At this point in time, I was doing better in my life those attacks (flashbacks) were in the past, thankfully. However, regaining my sense of self again was also a process. I once had learning disabilities, but now felt I had strong learning disabilities, as I was trying to regain myself and get my life back.

I was regaining in using areas within better then when I became sick. This journey was my first memory and also the journey up to Purgatory/Heaven twice and also of me taking in all that I can discover. This is what worked, despite me having my learning disabilities and I wanted to share it with others.

Why I attempted going into college. I was recovered at this time over my second trauma and I had lost my job due to the economy dropping. Thankfully, it was at this point that I was able to at least attempt taking the tests to get into college and have a chance passing. My learning disabilities prohibited this for me early on, but through the writing of my son's book (not finished just yet) and having a friend from my past read it, she pointed out some things like I write backwards. Why do I put the end at the beginning and beginning at the end? I also was not good with spelling and it still messes me up even today, lol. However, I was able to get into college. Hurrah! I just passed the English class, failed the Computer class and had to take this Introduction to Computers class. The course I had taken was Graphic Arts. I had only one other class to take in order to get my degree, but this class I knew I couldn't succeed due to my learning disabilities. I feel blessed and forever grateful to have had wonderful teachers that were understanding and guided me through on my college journey.

Later on, I revisited my younger years to find a reason in doing so. I have a child and in his early years he was one that couldn't sit still. As a baby, he was very alert and aware and once he began to crawl I noticed a change. It was only when he crawled that he became unreachable often. Once he began to walk on his own, that changed from when he crawled and now it seemed all the time, he couldn't sit still nor learn.

I never revisited my younger years to help my son because he was now hyper and unreachable, as well unreachable from one year of age on through the next few years. I didn't pick up the fact that we had *some* similarities; this comes later in his years. He was diagnosed with Sensory issues (Dysfunction), Auditory Processing issues and multiple learning disabilities and eventually diagnosed with Autism. Today in his early 20's he has Autism plus Asperger's Syndrome (he flip flops higher and lower intelligence) and has Sensory Dysfunction. His Autism and Asperger levels both I personally believe, witnessing countless times where it can affect his Sensory Dysfunction causing his Sensory to rise high and also can be reversed where his Sensory

Dysfunction if rising can increase his issues with his Autism and Asperger's Syndrome.

My counselor discovered a huge piece to my puzzle that she finds in the ending of my worst moments (lasted three weeks). Several years ago, she did bring this up to me, yet I didn't see this connection at that time and I let this thought go. Only this time it registered and made perfect, logical sense as I recalled moments spotted through my son, made me get it this time. This opened the doorway towards my recovery and resolving occurred, made it possible to ever have had a full recovery, I did! The timing, some might say is a coincidence, however, I know it wasn't. I caught in her discovery, the key piece that removed despair from me instantly.

It was like someone had "poured water over my head" type moment. It was that quick. I began writing my son's journey about his disabilities; my discoveries spotted through him to be passed onto the medical field for further research and discovered I was having some similarities. For example, like Auditory Processing complications and after going through PTSD and the fact that I recovered, I am adding more of my journey of discoveries in his book. This book is not out yet, but will mention the name of this book.

The book I am working on will be called "This Special Life and Us" volume 2

Back tracking. When I asked Jesus what I will be when I grow up, he answered only "Designer". (I made some attempts in the past with no avail.) Back in 2000, I was in pursuit once again to discover and become this "Designer", Jesus spoke of. Only I didn't know how this was going to come about. My son with his issues, and him not able to fall asleep yet in his bed, began sleeping now in mine instead of my mom's. My dad slept on his recliner in the family room. It was my mom's grand idea he needing another near so he began sleeping with her. Trust me, she regretted it after awhile. I sat in the dark for up to three whole hours, what a nightmare trying to get him to stay in the bed, yet alone fall asleep. All I had was my thoughts to occupy me, when not focused on returning him back to bed. I began using this somewhat quiet time and be constructive with it. I returned to what Jesus told me what I will be, "Designer". I ruled out drawing, I couldn't draw, so I thought. What I began doing was visualizing a fashion design in my head, and the more I did this the better I got at it. I was seeing new designs I not seen out there and felt hopeful, only overtime I became frustrated because I can't just describe what I see within my thoughts to another. Overtime, speaking with Jesus over my huge dilemma I resolved to draw. My first drawing attempt was awful, literally. I was discouraged for awhile. I felt I had to try at least one more time, promising Jesus I will give 100%, and if I don't see any improvement I will not return to this as a pathway. This time I only focused on the design itself, an outfit, not adding a person wearing it. WOW! I had seen some improvement, showing hope in this pathway. I was excited I gave it another try. I drew almost every night, while my son watched his cartoon. First I focused on drawing all the idea designs I had prior come up with in my head. I began just drawing and sought for discoveries as I drew. (Ex; a pair of pants and discovered a different form of pants idea). At this stage, my passion for discovery opened wide. Most of my drawings were of discoveries I can discover. I was experiencing such a natural high. Odd as this sounds, paper to me was precious, and refused to throw out a drawing, instead I focused to discover something, and always did. I am not saying this discovery was a home run, but still was a new discovery and was charged up in moving forward. These designs were the work I told God I was going to burn. I still wasn't doing this for a living, nor knew how to get them to be seen. My own limitation with knowledge was holding me back in this field, with how to, fell short in taking the next steps. I was frustrated, and felt extremely discouraged. On top of this I began seeing some of my designs coming out through another designer, yet still I didn't burn my designs I worked so hard creating. Today, still they've gone nowhere. I still feel the pressure by God to somehow do something with these. Later, the recession hit and I was guided to take Graphic Arts.

We all are given gifts and blessings from God to be using. These blessing, these gifts God has given to me; I shared some of my story in the hope that it will help or comfort others!

From my first memory, I caught on to this message that God is God for all. God is love. As well, I learned that God offers all to include seeing him as being "Father," yet never forgetting Him, as always being He is God! "God is the Father over all called Father, therefore Father to all." Some years later I also learned this through Jesus. He had spoken all these very things, as in the Prayer He taught when He was here, "Our Father who art in Heaven…" What I grew in learning early on (as well later) is that God is Merciful for all, (even those that offenses may be great, He awaits for these some). God is Love, as a father is (or should be as). God is Merciful, as a father is (or should be as).

There are many that formed personal relationships (or acknowledged) God, as well as many that formed personal relationships (or acknowledged) Jesus. Some might look to Him as a Prophet of His time and some see Him as being the Son of God.

Some choose to not acknowledge either of them at all throughout the ages. (This is one's right to their choosing, I get and respect). I have respect of other's right in having their own faith and that we all work in getting along with one another.

I am sharing some of what I experienced while through my own due was by Jesus taking me up to Heaven those two times. He is aware of my eagerness to share this to all others was not shown or told couldn't while there. I feel on one point being made is that each of us are equal (united) and could agree upon, as is each of us will experience and we all will leave here on this earth and I pass onto you two ways that were shown to me and what I was allowed to see while up there.

The End!

I just learned of this and thought to pass on, this is the 100th anniversary Our Lady of Fatima apparitions (2017), that she appeared at Lourdes to three children passing on a message.

A preview "This Special Life and Us" volume 2

My anger, frustration, and confusion surrounded me all due to my ignorance and God and Jesus working through my own son's journey as they worked through me to help my son, God and Jesus helped me.

This is my journey of understanding and learning of my son's disabilities with God and Jesus very much a part in. I am not a doctor, nor am I a therapist. I am a mom who figured out how to get her son to return when both mind and body were shutting down (as inaccessible) inside of him. I became educated in many areas of learning disabilities through his journey. Learning about him has added to my own understanding in his older childhood of some of my learning disabilities. This led to huge insights and discoveries, many blessings from God, Jesus and the Holy Spirit in union with them the whole while that we both received. I asked them to help me bring my son to his 100% and they have shown me an odd unique pathway which opened doors for his growth in moving forward. I share both our journeys (my older years having had Post Traumatic Stress Disorder, recovered) in hope God may open more doors for many in need of healing as well. I believe it was my obligation to share our journeys and document everything I could remember.

I am presenting them for the necessity of many purposes. The main reason is hopefully will help others, whether it is in a small way or a big way, and is for the Medical Board for further study. Another reason is for the school boards, Doctors and staff, Teachers, Therapists. I will be able to draw from what I do share within this book as I present my strong comments, opinions, and suggestions and my discoveries which brought about my massive theories both taken from my son and my own journey *only* for consideration for the Medical Board and the Foundation of Sensory for further review. The first is for others to hear his journey, hopefully might connect with or learn and grow in inspiring other adults in helping their young children and possibly changes in which might occur. I am only a mom who raised a son that had a lot going wrong for him and was making it right! No one has my permission to use anything from my book without my permission. However one can seek guidance and counsel through their doctor.

Prologue

My sons' birth

As I begin our journey I will take you to a time when I was seven months pregnant and mention the turn of events. I went to a club to help my close friend celebrate her daughter's 21st birthday. There was a band, and the music was extremely loud. The noise caused me concern for my unborn baby. I moved further away. After moving as far away as I could, I felt my son turn in my belly. He was checked out by the doctor and they found no stress, I was reassured that he was fine even though he was breach. Two weeks prior to my son's scheduled delivery date my doctor said he could try to turn my baby. That was an experience in itself, it wasn't painful, but certainly a bizarre experience. During this experience, I was told I could go into labor early during this and that I should be prepared with my bag and my labor coach. I was mentally ready for his arrival should I go into labor at this time. I agreed to try but it was unsuccessful. Although it did not happen that day, he did come early.

I welcome you to my bad "hair" brain day. I was entering into the realm of many new moms on their special day. This was my moment to shine, to show I am cool, collected and definitely in control. Oh yes! I now arrived into the ranks of many new moms to be, where you're totally out of character. Reasoning decided to take a walk and being out of control is an understatement. I was in denial. I was in labor. This was not a good thing considering the hospital was 30 minutes away, and my son remained breach. Earlier in the day, I had eaten pepperoni pizza with my family. Shortly after they left, the pizza wasn't agreeing with me. Waves of stomach cramps would pass and then I would be fine. A couple of hours had passed with cramps coming and going. I decided to give my doctor a call. Maybe he could prescribe something that would alleviate my discomfort so that I either will be sick or stop this feeling. My Doctor informed me it sounded like I was in labor. I told him that I do not think so. I was a bit stubborn, thinking surely this could not be labor pains, keep in mind that this was my first pregnancy. The little voice inside my head was confirming what the doctor said, "yes, I was in labor". My poor doctor and I were now at a standstill. (To be continued…)